NESTBOXES
YOUR COMPLETE GUIDE

BY DAVID CROMACK

BTO
Looking out for birds

First published in 2018 British Trust for Ornithology
www.bto.org | info@bto.org

First published in 2018
British Trust for Ornithology
The Nunnery, Thetford, Norfolk, IP24 2PU
01842 750050
www.bto.org | info@bto.org
Registered Charity Number 216652 (England & Wales), SC039193 (Scotland)

ISBN 978-1-908581-84-6
© British Trust for Ornithology

Designed by: Tom Sayer Design | www.tomsayerdesign.co.uk

Printed by: Printer Trento, Italy

Front cover: Nuthatch, Blue Tit, Great Tit chicks: David Tipling / Wren: NE Wildlife
Back cover: Nick Baker: Mike Alsford / Great Tit: David Tipling / Illustration: Nigel Hawtin

All rights reserved. No part of this publication may be reproduced, stored in an electronic
retrieval system, or transmitted in any form or by any means, electronic, mechanical, internet,
photocopying, recording or otherwise, without the prior written permission of the publisher and
copyright holders. Neither the publisher nor the authors can accept liability for the use of any
of the materials or methods recommended in this book or for any consequences arising out
of their use, nor can they be held responsible for any errors or omissions that may be found in
the text or may occur at a future date as a result of changes in rules, laws or equipment.

Environment: The paper used for this book has been certified as coming from well-managed
forests and other controlled sources according to the rules of the Forest Stewardship Council.

This book was printed and bound in Italy by Printer Trento, an FSC ® certified company for
printing books on FSC mixed papers in compliance with the chain of custody and on-product
labelling standards. Printer Trento has an ISO 14001 certified environmental management system.

"THE BIG THING THAT'S MISSING
FROM TODAY'S MANICURED PARKS AND
GARDENS IS HOLES. NO HOLES
MEANS NO HOLE-NESTING BIRDS.
PUTTING A BOX UP SIMPLY REPLACES WHAT
HUMANS HAVE TAKEN AWAY."

———————————

NICK BAKER, NATURALIST & WILDLIFE
TELEVISION PRESENTER

CONTENTS

48–71

NESTBOXES WITH SMALL ENTRANCE HOLES

10–47

ALL YOU NEED TO KNOW ABOUT NESTBOXES

72–81

NESTBOXES WITH MEDIUM-SIZED ENTRANCE HOLES

BRITAIN NEEDS MORE HOLES

By Naturalist & Wildlife Television Presenter Nick Baker

The briefest glance around Poland's ancient Białowieża Forest reminds me about our own island's past. With its towering oak and tangled underscrub it feels more like a rainforest than the woodlands I'm used to back home.

Here's where life clings onto life in an interconnecting web, pulsing with vibrant verdancy. But for every sprouting limb and towering bole, there's a dead branch, a knothole and a giant fallen carcass. If every conservation manager, forest worker and gardener could visit this place just once it would stay with them for the rest of their lives.

Białowieża is the last fragment of the great wild wood that once stretched across Northern Europe. It's an intoxicating place, full of age-old natural wisdom. Wild in the truest sense, it's where many creatures that once roamed our own islands are still found. Wolf, European Beaver, Wild Boar, European Bison and Brown Bear coexist with the more familiar Blue Tit, Blackbird, Hedgehog and Common Shrew.

Look into the dark, gleaming eye of a garden Robin and you're looking into the eye

"Think back to all those natural cavities that would have existed in the wild woods standing where your garden is now. Every bird box represents a missing piece of that ancient natural architecture. And you really can't put up too many of the things."

of something every bit as wild as the Wild Boar it once followed around the forest. It's easy to forget the place of these tamed, familiar friends in a much bigger wilderness picture.

And as my senses absorb the richness of the ancient Polish landscape, what stands out isn't just the interwoven tapestry of animal and plant life, but the sheer number of holes. In Białowieża they're everywhere: rot holes, hollow boughs, crevices, fungus-softened hearts, ivy clad branches and fern-swathed boughs aplenty.

In risk-averse Britain, of course, we're so obsessed with things dropping off or falling over we panic and call a tree surgeon. As a direct consequence of this over-managing – and historic felling of our ancient woodlands – we're left with few trees of a maturity for holes to exist.

Last spring I was making nestboxes with some college students, using patterns from this very book as it happens. We put up eight boxes: within weeks, six were stuffed with dog hair, sheep's wool, moss, feathers and even yellow fluff from some lost

tennis ball. And nestled deep in every soft mass were clutches of tiny speckled off-white eggs, with a female Blue Tit patiently sitting on each of them.

To find so many boxes occupied was a welcome reward for our efforts. But the hidden message is even more important. The big thing that's missing from today's manicured parks and gardens is holes. No holes means no hole-nesting birds. And as you've figured by now, putting a box up simply replaces what humans have taken away.

So think back to all those natural cavities that would have existed in the wild woods standing where your garden is now. Every bird box represents a missing piece of that ancient natural architecture. And you really can't put up too many of the things – whether it's a classic box with a hole, a tea chest for an owl, a wedge-shaped box for Treecreepers or an open-fronted box for Robins, flycatchers and thrushes.

Nick Baker

ALL YOU NEED TO KNOW ABOUT NESTBOXES

◀

NESTBOXES WITH SMALL ENTRANCE HOLES

NESTBOXES WITH MEDIUM-SIZED ENTRANCE HOLES

NESTBOXES WITH LARGE ENTRANCE HOLES

SMALL OPEN-FRONTED NESTBOXES

SPECIALIST NESTBOXES

MORE ABOUT NESTBOXES

AN INTRODUCTION TO NESTBOXES

Changes to the British landscape have generally been for the benefit of humans, not wildlife. Finding suitable natural nesting sites has become increasingly difficult for many species of bird, so providing nestboxes can make a big difference.

Just why do British birds need nestboxes?

For thousands of years birds have been able to use holes in trees, crevices in rocks and even Rabbit holes as safe places to lay eggs and raise young, so why do we need to worry?

Well, birds deserve a helping hand from humans because over centuries the UK population has surged to the point where our activities have an impact – so often negative – on all other forms of life.

For instance, look what we've done to our forests. After the passing of the last Ice Age, Britain was covered in a broad range of woodland plants and trees, meaning there was no shortage of nesting opportunities for resident and migrant bird species. As our ancestors moved from hunting and gathering to farming, land was cleared to make way for crops. The loss of woodland and forest cover reduced opportunities for cavity-nesting species, although it also created new opportunities for open-country species.

By the time the Normans arrived in 1066 forest cover was just 15%, falling further to just 5% by 1905. Thankfully, the losses were halted and re-planting has lifted England's forest cover back to 13%. Though encouraging, many other European countries average far more, so we should do whatever we can to make up for the shortfall.

Hedgerows have traditionally been important for nesting birds and as wildlife corridors, but many have been removed as part of the move to more intensive agriculture. EU legislation to encourage more environmentally-friendly farming has meant the trend has slowed down since the 1980s, but in some parts of the country 50% of hedgerows have gone, while others are so badly managed that their value to wildlife is reduced.

A survey of hedgerow changes revealed that between 1984 and 1990 hedgerow length in England had declined by 20% and in Wales by 25%. While outright removal of hedgerows accounted for 9,500 km per year, almost half of the loss was a result of lack of management.

The continuing need to build more houses, plus shifting weather patterns triggered by climate change, will place more pressures on breeding birds. Inevitably the loss of bird-friendly habitats in the general countryside has led to serious declines in the populations of many species, so they need all the help they can get.

The good news is that every family in the land can do something positive for wildlife without straining the budget. If you'd like to 'do your bit', the garden is a great place to start. The British Trust for Ornithology (BTO) reckons that if all the gardens in Britain were rolled up into one giant plot, it would have an area bigger than the county of Suffolk. Just imagine what an impact it would have for birds if each of our gardens contained one or

▲ Once secure, this open-fronted nestbox will be concealed with ivy and other foliage to protect the nest from predation.

more nestboxes and a range of plants and invertebrates to provide food for hungry birds.

The primary aim of this book is to encourage more people to make nestboxes of varying designs and to provide information about siting and maintenance to increase bird breeding success.

In this guide, you'll find:
- Tips on making your garden a wildlife-friendly zone.
- Which species you can attract to use garden nestboxes.
- The best designs for nestboxes and step-by-step building instructions.
- How to site nestboxes successfully.
- How to protect nesting birds from cats and other predators.
- What materials are best to use.
- What tools you will need.
- When to erect your nestboxes.
- Information on nestbox care and maintenance.
- A buyer's guide to ready-made nestboxes and refuges for animals and amphibians.
- Links to organisations involved in helping nesting birds.

THE WIDER BENEFITS OF NESTBOX SCHEMES

Nestboxes have the power to encourage community spirit and enhance wildlife interest. As they are fairly easy to produce, you could engage volunteers from schools, bird clubs, adult education groups, wildlife reserves and University of the Third Age members. Sponsorship from a local timber merchant or other company can keep down the costs of buying materials and the proceeds of nestbox sales could be donated to worthy local causes.

Finally, the therapeutic benfit of nestboxes should not be underestimated. There are an increasing number of studies that show that physical activity and exposure to green spaces can overcome mental stress, while simply being able to watch birds visiting nestboxes will lift the spirits of housebound elderly or disabled residents.

The primary aim of this book is to encourage more people to make nestboxes of varying designs and to provide information about siting and maintenance to increase bird breeding success.

THE VALUE OF MONITORING

How well birds do at raising a brood of chicks can influence the numbers of individuals entering the breeding population in future years. We know, for example, that poor breeding success in Sparrowhawks – caused by pesticide pollution – led to a decline in the UK Sparrowhawk population. By monitoring the breeding attempts made in your nestboxes you can contribute valuable information to help scientists understand why bird populations are changing. You can find out how to monitor your nestboxes safely later on in this book (pp 149-150).

THINGS TO NOTE

The templates we provide are for the simplest and most straightforward designs and should be manageable for anyone with rudimentary carpentry skills. If you lack a suitable working space and the tools needed for DIY boxes, there is always the option of buying ready-made nestboxes from the many companies supplying the garden bird trade.

The designs cater for the most common garden birds, plus a few, such as Tawny Owl and Redstart, that occur less frequently in domestic gardens. The guide does not claim to be the last word in nestboxes, even though it draws on the experience of BTO members and others, spanning more than 80 years. The BTO welcomes further suggestions, designs and knowledge accrued from practical experience in order to enhance future editions of the book.

You will notice that some of the nestboxes in our photographs do not match the standard design template.

▲ The extra-deep entrance hole on this nestbox chosen by a Blue Tit offers additional protection from squirrel attacks.

This is deliberate, because birds are very adaptable and will use a wide range of design variations. So, feel free to adapt a design to suit the wood you have to hand rather than paying for expensive new materials.

Designs may also need to be modified to take into account local requirements such as prevailing weather, high levels of predator activity and availability of materials. Some species may prefer a particular design in one location but choose something different elsewhere. A good example is Tawny Owl, which occasionally opts for a chimney-style box over the standard box with large entrance hole.

Be prepared for your first nestboxes to be ignored.

While some prospecting Robins may inspect a box within an hour or so and take to it quickly, another box may remain unused for a couple of years. If there are no takers after that period of time, it is worth trying a new position.

A comprehensive guide to all species that will use nestboxes would be a large and unwieldy publication, so this book concentrates on birds most likely to be found in gardens and woodlands. On pages 138 to 141 you can find an extended list of UK birds that have been known to use nestboxes and other man-made structures, such as floating rafts, and for more information on constructing these, please visit the BTO website (www.bto.org).

NESTBOXES WITHIN A WILDLIFE-FRIENDLY GARDEN

A nestbox won't work well in isolation, so ensure its surroundings
are as wildlife-friendly as possible. Use this guide to test how
good your garden is for visiting birds and other creatures.

Your decision to make and install bird nestboxes is
most likely to pay dividends if your garden or other chosen
location is part of a habitat that is managed to benefit
wildlife in all its forms. How wildlife-friendly is your plot?
Here's a checklist of things to consider:

- Soil and compost
- Plants for pollen/nectar
- Plants for berries and fruit
- Plants for shelter and protection
- Wildlife refuges
- Water
- Food and feeder hygeine

SOIL AND COMPOST

A healthy garden starts at ground level with soil that
is free of chemical pesticides and herbicides.

Seeing your lettuce patch ravaged by slugs can be
frustrating, but remember that Common Toads and
Hedgehogs feed on some species and if you can tolerate
living with snails they may attract hungry Song Thrushes
into your garden.

Hoverflies, lacewings and ladybirds will all eat insect
pests, and will be attracted to your garden by the
presence of flowers, shrubs, sheltered corners and even
water – many hoverfly larvae live in water.

Making your own compost is one of the most positive
contributions you can make to encourage biodiversity and
minimise the amount of waste you send to landfill. It is hard
to overstate the benefits that stem from composting. Not
only will it reduce your reliance on chemical fertilisers, but
compost speeds up the natural recycling of nutrients while
also improving soil structure and water retention.

Examine the lower levels of your compost bin and
you'll find a complete zoo of worms, beetles, slugs, snails,
woodlice and other invertebrates all contributing to the
breakdown of plant material. Equally important to this
composting process, but not so visible, are fungi and
bacteria. If you are very lucky, the heat generated inside
a compost heap may attract a Slow-worm or Grass Snake.

Creating your own compost is the environmentally-
friendly thing to do, because it means you don't have
to buy commercial soil improvers which need plastic
packaging and add to air pollution while being transported
to your nearest garden centre.

For smaller suburban gardens, a recycled plastic compost
bin is the most practical option as it takes up less space
than compost heaps that are open to the elements. Many
local councils have schemes to subsidise the cost of buying
bins, most of which have a door at the bottom for extracting
the fully rotted plant material more easily.

COLOURFUL FLORAL ATTRACTIONS
Planting a wide variety of nectar-rich flowering plants not only adds colour to the garden, but will help to feed beautiful butterflies such as this Peacock, plus a host of pollinating bees and hoverflies.

PLANTS FOR POLLEN AND NECTAR

Insects are not only valuable pollinators, but are part of the food chain for birds, amphibians, mammals and other insects. Your choice of garden plants can ensure that there is a supply of nectar and pollen-rich flowers on offer to butterflies, bees, hoverflies and other insects for most of the year. The insects will repay your generosity by fertilising other plants to ensure a continuing supply of seeds and fruit.

The early part of the year can be a problem for insects seeking flowers from which to feed. You can help by planting flowers that provide early season nectar. If you have the space, some *Mahonia* bushes will prove a great asset. Their heavily-scented yellow flower spikes are a magnet for insects and later in the year the dark blue berries will attract Blackbirds, Song Thrushes and maybe even a migrant Blackcap.

If you plant your *Mahonia* close to a wall you can use its Holly-like spiky evergreen leaves to protect an open-type nestbox from raiding cats, squirrels and other bird predators.

Don't be seduced by those plant cultivars which have been developed to produce big or double flowers, as most of them generate little pollen or nectar. Conventional wisdom suggests that native plant species have the greatest benefits for wildlife, but exotics such as *Buddleia* (originally imported from North America) and *Hebe* (native to New Zealand, the Falklands and South America) are well worth a place in your garden.

One native plant that is not generally welcome in gardens is Common Nettle, especially if there are children likely to come into contact with its stinging leaves, but if you have an out-of-the-way patch you might consider keeping it for its value to insects. Butterflies such as Small Tortoiseshell, Peacock and Comma, plus a range of moths, will all lay eggs on nettles and their caterpillars use the leaves as food. One way to keep this plant under control is to harvest some of its leaf stems, which contain a lot of nitrogenous compounds, to make a liquid fertiliser or as a compost activator.

RECOMMENDED PLANTS FOR POLLEN AND NECTAR

As a result of its long-running Plants for Bugs study, the Royal Horticultural Society has a great deal of useful advice on the best bird and insect-friendly plants for pollen, nectar and seeds. Here are some you can try.

LAVENDER *Lavendula*:
Elephant Hawk-moth is an unusual visitor to Lavender, but the scent will attract a constant succesion of bees, hoverflies and butterflies when in flower throughout the summer.

SUNFLOWER *Helianthus*:
Sunflowers' pollen-rich flowers benefit insects, but later in the year the plant provides seed for birds such as Greenfinch.

HONEYSUCKLE *Lonicera*:
The native version *(Lonicera periclymenum)* of this climbing plant has one of the sweetest perfumes of any plant. It is particularly strong at night in order to attract a wide variety of pollinating moths, including the spectacular Hummingbird Hawk-moth. Bumblebees find the flower nectar irresistible and White Admiral caterpillars feed exclusively on the plant. Dormice are known to feed on its fruit and you can expect to see birds such as Bullfinches eating the juicy berries in autumn.

THYME *Thymus*:
This aromatic herb is a favourite with cooks, but its nectar also attracts bees, hoverflies and other pollinators. As it matures and spreads, the woody stems of thyme create cover for beetles and other invertebrates.

FOXGLOVE *Digitalis*:
Though poisonous to humans and pets, this traditional cottage garden plant is eaten by the caterpillars of at least two moth species and its pink, bell-like flowers will be abuzz with bees between June and September.

PURPLE LOOSESTRIFE *Lythrum salicaria*:
A pink wildflower that prospers in damper soil, it flowers from June until the end of August, providing an important nectar source for long-tongued insects including Brimstones, Red-tailed Bumblebees and Elephant Hawk-moths.

ICE PLANT *Hylotelephium spectabile*:
This form of Sedum produces large flower heads on long stems and will produce nectar for bees and butterflies during the autumn season.

COMPOST BIN OPTIONS
Above: Bins made from recycled plastic
are the best option if you have limited
space in your garden, but larger open
heaps (right) convert vegetable matter
to compost much more speedily.

PLANTS FOR BERRIES AND FRUIT

Most soft fruits such as raspberries, blueberries and strawberries will be targeted by birds, so protect your crops by making sure they are adequately netted. Choose small-mesh fabric or plastic nets because Blackbirds and other birds can easily get tangled in the softer string nets. Woodpigeons can be a persistent problem to fruit-growers as they will easily break the tops off plants due to their weight, so erect your netting well above your bushes.

If you have a large garden it is well worth considering planting apple or crab apple trees. Not only will you have a crop for yourself, but windfall fruit will be appreciated by birds.

Plants you can grow to offer birds an alternative food source include Rowan (*Sorbus aucuparia*). Commonly known as the Mountain Ash because it grows well at higher altitudes, the Rowan is not related to Ash trees. As it usually reaches 5-12 m in height, it is not suitable for very small gardens, but if you have the space you'll find its crop of autumn berries will attract a constant stream of feeding

thrushes, including Scandinavian visitors such as Fieldfare and Redwing. In exceptional winters, if the berries have not already been gobbled up, Waxwings may pay a visit to feed.

Choose a variety with red berries as the orange and yellow ones don't have the same pulling power for birds. Several moth caterpillars, including the Autumn Green Carpet eat the leaves, while caterpillars of the Apple Fruit Moth feed on the berries.

PLANTS FOR SHELTER AND PROTECTION

Spend time watching birds come to your feeders and you'll soon realise that they all seek to minimise the time they spend out in the open. Coal, Great and Blue Tits will all take Sunflower seeds from the feeder to a nearby tree or shrub where they feel safe to remove the hard shell and consume the food. Research has shown that dominant species and older individuals favour feeders closer to cover, forcing subordinate or inexperienced individuals to feed in more exposed locations where the risk of predation

▲ Scandinavian Waxwings visit the UK when winter food supplies run low: berry-bearing bushes may tempt them into your garden.

is greater. To create a safe environment for visiting birds it make sense to plant a few thorny bushes within easy reach of your bird feeders.

Firethorn *(Pyracantha)*: The spiky nature of this dense shrub provides great protection for nesting birds and once planted it needs very little attention. It can cope with both exposed positions and shade and gives wildlife a further helping hand with berries and nectar.

Hawthorn *(Crataegus monogyna)*: One plant that really underlines the value of native species is the Hawthorn which can support more than 300 invertebrate species. It is the foodplant for many moth caterpillars, while Its flowers provide nectar and pollen for bees and other pollinating insects. The red autumn fruit, known as haws, are rich in antioxidants and are eaten by many migrating birds such as Redwings and Fieldfares as well as resident thrushes and small mammals. As part of a hedge its dense thorny foliage makes ideal nesting shelter for many species of bird. All these comments apply equally to Blackthorn *(Prunus spinosa)*.

Barberry *(Berberis)*: Native *Berberis* has green leaves, but varieties from other parts of the world feature dark red or purple leaves. The yellow flowers of all varieties provide nectar for butterflies and moths, while its sharp thorns offer small birds some protection when hiding from predators such as Sparrowhawks.

Ivy *(Hedera helix)*: If there is one plant that ticks all the boxes in terms of benefits to wildlife it has to be Ivy. Mature plants flower between September and November, providing nectar and pollen when other sources are running short. Ivy's dark berries have a very high fat content, making them great food for pigeons, thrushes and Blackcaps. This evergreen climber will cover walls and large tree trunks, making it a valuable hiding place for insects, bats, rodents and birds.

▲ A log pile in a damp part of your plot will soon have a thriving community of beetles and other insects living within it.

WILDLIFE REFUGES

A fallen tree that is allowed to decompose naturally becomes a valuable habitat in its own right for many different insects, a refuge and hunting ground for small mammals, reptiles and amphibians, and shelter for over-wintering and hibernating wildlife. Sadly, Britain has far fewer wooded areas than in the past so this resource is far rarer then it once was.

You can make your own contribution to limiting the loss by installing a log pile in your garden to support fungi, wood-boring insects, woodlice, beetle grubs and wood wasps. In turn, these insects become prey for spiders, frogs, toads, Hedgehogs and birds. It is possible that butterflies and ladybirds will take up residence in the drier parts of the wood pile over winter.

Bacteria and disease can be harboured in decaying logs, so it is sensible to position a log pile away from living trees in your garden. If honey fungus spreads to living trees and shrubs, it can kill them in a short space of time.

Source your logs from a local tree surgeon, rather than taking them from woodland where they may already be supporting a wildlife community. Hardwood logs of

▲ Birds like this Blackbird need to bathe regularly to keep feathers in good condition, so provide clean water at all times.

different lengths are better than softwood and ideally they should have the bark intact. Sink the lowest level of logs into the soil to keep them damp and scatter soil between each layer as you build upwards to help retain moisture and encourage decay.

Many suburban gardens are so manicured they hold very little value for wildlife. Curb your instinct to tidy up leaves, grasses and twigs from the flower bed; in spring they will be collected by many species of bird for nest material, while the hollow stems of perennials left in the border can be used by overwintering insects.

Thinking about building a rockery? You can provide hibernating reptiles and amphibians with secure underground refuges by arranging stones to create pockets of space out of sight of any predators and away from the worst winter weather. Amphibians prefer to hibernate in a cool (but not cold), dark and damp shelter, though some frogs use the mud at the bottom of ponds for this purpose.

THE IMPORTANCE OF WATER

It is hard to overstate the importance of water to wildlife, so give some thought on how you can provide a reliable source of this precious liquid. Even in the smallest backyards, there should be space for a formal bird bath, or even an up-turned dustbin lid set in the ground, where birds can drink or cleanse their feathers. However, bigger is better, so think about installing the biggest pool your plot will allow.

Think about location carefully before you start digging a pond, as it will be a lot of effort to move it to a better site later on. Most forms of wildlife respond best to warm, sunny conditions, so choose a spot that gets the sun for at least part of the day and definitely avoid putting your water feature under a large tree. It will fill the pond with leaves each autumn and growing roots may one day puncture the pool lining.

Ideally, there will be some reasonably mature shrubs and trees surrounding your chosen spot, so that birds, amphibians and mammals have some cover on their approach to the water. Putting native marginal plants into the water at pond edges will give perches and cover to wildlife – try Water Forget-me-not, Lesser Spearwort or Marsh Marigold in aquatic mesh plant pots filled with low nutrient soil and grit.

Your local garden centre will be happy to sell you pre-formed pond liners made from polyethyline or some other form of plastic, but if you want to have complete control over the size and shape of your water feature then a butyl liner is the option to go for. It is beyond the scope of this book to offer a step-by-step guide on how to construct a successful wildlife pond, but such information is available in the BTO book 'Gardening for Birdwatchers'.

One feature that should be considered an 'essential' no matter what type of liner you choose is to have at least one gradually sloping side so that birds and mammals can drink and bathe safely in shallow water. If your pond has hard edges on all sides, then construct a 'ladder' of stones and sticks so that any creature that accidentally falls in can make its escape.

To prevent the water freezing over completely in a hard winter, it is a good idea to make the lowest point of your pond at least 60cm deep, If possible, introduce shelves at varying depths to benefit the different wildlife which uses the pond.

Once the construction work has been completed, remove any soil that may have fallen into the pond liner,

because it will be rich in nutrients, so will encourage the growth of algae. Save rainwater for filling the pond because tap water contains many chemicals that will harm wildlife.

ALL-YEAR BIRD FEEDING AND FEEDER HYGIENE

As we have discussed, creating a healthy garden environment should ensure a food chain from the smallest insects right up to birds and hunting mammals, but sadly there is not always enough natural food available in the wider countryside. By setting up feeders for birds and mammals you will not only be giving them a helping hand but you'll increase your opportunities for viewing these visitors.

View the catalogues or websites of birdfood companies and you'll be amazed at the sheer inventiveness of the product range. The traditional offerings of peanuts, mixed seeds, sunflower seeds and hearts are now joined by salt-free peanut butter, fat balls with embedded seeds, plus meal worms and suet grains.

The choice of bird tables, window trays, rain guards, seed and nut feeders is growing all the time, so you will find it easy to create the perfect combination for the birds that regularly visit your garden, and that includes some ingenious devices to keep pest species, such as Grey Squirrels or Woodpigeons taking more than their fair share of provided food.

It is important to keep your feeders and bird baths clean to prevent the spread of disease among visiting birds. Equally, make sure you wear gloves when cleaning feeders.

You may be able to tempt Hedgehogs into your garden by putting out saucers of moist cat or dog food or cat biscuits. In low temperatures this type of food may freeze over, so switch to chopped-up unsalted peanuts. Under no circumstances put out bread and milk – Hedgehogs cannot digest bread and the milk will induce diarrhoea, sometimes with fatal results.

BIRDFEEDER ACTION

Small birds may struggle to find enough food in winter, so if you can provide good quality food on a regular basis, you may be treated to views of wonderful visitors such as Long-tailed Tits (main picture) and Greenfinches.

LOCATING & PROTECTING YOUR NESTBOX

Careful placement of nestboxes within your garden is needed to ensure that eggs and chicks do not suffer in adverse weather conditions and remain safe from cats and other predators.

PICKING THE IDEAL LOCATION FOR YOUR NESTBOX

While it may be tempting to fix a garden nestbox in a position where you and your family can observe it being used by birds, your top priority must be to provide a safe location where the chicks can be raised with minimal risk from predators or bad weather.

All boxes should be positioned so that maintenance and cleaning is made as easy as possible. If you intend to inspect the nest and monitor its contents, make sure you can do this easily and with a minimum of disruption to the parent birds.

In addition to these general considerations, certain species may have specific preferences, making an ideal situation for one species completely unsuitable for another. Check the individual species accounts for more information.

Nestboxes are most urgently needed in places where natural holes are scarce but where food is plentiful. For instance, have a look around your neighbourhood for managed woods where mature trees are cropped and dead wood removed. Other options are farmland where mature trees have been removed from hedgerows, forest plantations where trees are not big enough to have developed holes, and finally your own back garden.

Once you've identified a suitable location, there are three key factors to keep in mind when positioning your nestbox – prevailing weather conditions, deterring predators and selecting the correct height for individual species.

Beating the weather – Ideally the entrance to your nestbox will be sheltered from the prevailing wind, rain and strong sunlight. Certainly your patio sun-trap will not be suitable because prolonged exposure to the sun's heat can cause young chicks within a nestbox to overheat and die.

If your garden is not shaded by surrounding trees or buildings, it will be best to angle the entrance hole in a northerly or easterly direction as these are usually facing away from prevailing wind and rain. A useful way to work out the main direction of rain in your area is to see which side of the trees have the greatest amount of green algae on the bark.

If you intend to place the box in deep, cold woodland, then you will need to adopt a different policy, setting the nestbox entrance to face south-east so that it will catch some early morning warmth from the sun.

In woodlands, your priority should be finding a sloping tree surface that allows you to tilt the box so that it faces slightly downwards to prevent rain entering through the entrance hole. If all the trees are resolutely upright, fix a batten to the back of the box to make it tilt downwards.

▲ Nestboxes at lower levels need to be hidden as much as possible to thwart attacks by predators.

Choosing the correct height – For many species the height of a box is not critically important – after all, in the wild they have to take natural holes where they find them. In your own garden it means you have the freedom to site the box low enough to clean easily or inspect. In more public places you might prefer to put the box up high, out of reach of vandals or inquisitive children.

For most species, the nestbox needs to be sited to allow a clear flight path. See the individual species accounts for detailed guidance on preferred heights.

Reducing the risk from predators – It is almost impossible to stop some predators, such as Weasels, finding and raiding nestboxes, but in your garden you can take a few steps to deter commoner pests such as cats and Grey Squirrels. See page 31 for more details.

HOW MANY BOXES SHOULD YOU PUT IN YOUR GARDEN?

The answer to this question depends not only on the size of your plot and the habitat, but also on what nesting species you are hoping to attract. Anyone lucky enough to own or have access to a large country estate, could start with 10 assorted and evenly-spaced small boxes per hectare. If these are all occupied, then keep adding boxes each breeding season until some remain unused.

For a more typical back yard plot (say 40 metres x 40 metres), you can start with three or four boxes: try an open box for a Robin as well as the small entrance hole boxes for tits. Space out the boxes to avoid aggressive territorial behaviour between close neighbours.

If your target birds are communal nesters such as Starlings or House Sparrows, then box density can be increased. Wall-mounted large boxes divided into two or three compartments may be adopted by sparrows but the best option for this species are individual boxes about one metre apart. For Starlings it is best to locate boxes on separate poles, trees or walls at different heights, but all reasonably close to each other.

THE BEST TIME TO INSTALL A NESTBOX

Traditionally, boxes for tits and other small birds are put up in early spring before the start of a new breeding season. Indeed, National Nest Box Week always starts on February 14 (St Valentine's Day) when birds are reputed to start their courtship. In reality, some species will be prospecting for nest sites long before this date. Juvenile birds may even begin to select potential sites during their first autumn and winter as they familiarise themselves with their local area.

Boxes which are in place by the autumn may well be used as roosting havens in extremely cold winter periods, so the best advice is to fix your box as soon as it is ready; after all, how many unused nestboxes lie in garden sheds, waiting for that 'ideal moment'? Do it now!

WHEN SHOULD NESTBOXES BE MOVED?

Your local birds may not rush to occupy a small box as soon as it is fixed in place, but generally you should have success in years two or three. If there is no interest after that, the birds are telling you something is wrong with the site, so it will pay to move the box to another location. For the larger boxes, it may be up to six years before they are adopted, so you'll need to be patient.

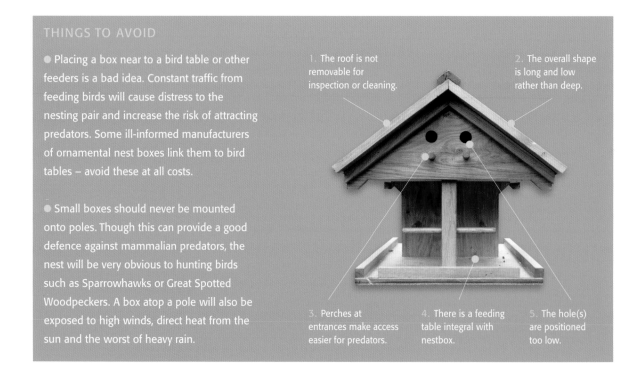

THINGS TO AVOID

● Placing a box near to a bird table or other feeders is a bad idea. Constant traffic from feeding birds will cause distress to the nesting pair and increase the risk of attracting predators. Some ill-informed manufacturers of ornamental nest boxes link them to bird tables – avoid these at all costs.

● Small boxes should never be mounted onto poles. Though this can provide a good defence against mammalian predators, the nest will be very obvious to hunting birds such as Sparrowhawks or Great Spotted Woodpeckers. A box atop a pole will also be exposed to high winds, direct heat from the sun and the worst of heavy rain.

1. The roof is not removable for inspection or cleaning.

2. The overall shape is long and low rather than deep.

3. Perches at entrances make access easier for predators.

4. There is a feeding table integral with nestbox.

5. The hole(s) are positioned too low.

FIX BOXES TO WALLS AND BUILDINGS

Putting a box on a building or wall is simpler than fixing it to a tree. Not only will your ladder be more secure when positioned against a wall, you will not have to worry about the tree growing and displacing the nestbox in future years. Screws or nails can be used for fixing boxes to buildings:

NAIL OPTIONS

● To attach a box to a brick wall, you will need to use masonry nails. These are specially hardened to penetrate mortar or soft brick without bending.

● To attach a box to a wooden structure, such as a barn, garage or shed, the ideal nail will be made from galvanised steel or copper, which will last far longer than metals that rust or corrode easily.

SCREW OPTIONS

● You will need a power drill and rawlplugs in order to fix a box to a brick wall using screws. It is worth making the extra effort, because long screws are less likely to work loose over time compared to nails. Again, choose stainless steel or brass screws to avoid long-term rust problems. Think ahead to the time

▲ Boxes should be tilted forward to prevent rain entering. For Swifts you can opt to fix external boxes (bottom left) or ones that are incorporated into the building.

you might want to remove a box for repair – if you smear the screws with oil before inserting they will be much easier to unscrew.

If you are planning an extension for your house or need to replace a roof,

there is the opportunity to incorporate bird boxes for species such as Swift and Barn Owl directly into the roof space of the new structure (see section on nestbox construction for more details – page 43).

HOW TO...

FIX BOXES TO TREES

Tree leaves and branches offer more shelter and concealment from potential predators than walls or buildings, but boxes attached to trees will require regular attention to keep them in good condition and securely fixed.

NAIL OPTIONS
● Fixing a horizontal batten to the back of your box helps to keep it away from rain running down the trunk of the tree. To prevent the batten splitting, first drill small holes through it before beginning to hammer in the nails. If you opt to nail the batten to a tree, be aware that nails will be squeezed out of the trunk as the tree grows, so you will need to inspect annually and re-fix if

the box has become loose. Use flat-headed nails as these will be pushed out with the batten as the tree grows, rather than being pulled through it.

● Avoid steel nails which will rust. Aluminium roofing nails, which have large flat heads are ideal, but it is also possible to buy nylon or plastic composite nails via the internet. It is important that you remove any metal nails or screws when the box is removed to avoid possible accidents with chainsaws later in the tree's life.

SCREW OPTIONS
● Stainless steel or brass screws are again the best choice to avoid issues with rust. Slacken them occasionally to allow for the tree's growth.

TYING OPTIONS
● You can choose to fix the box to a tree with wire, but it will need to be examined annually to check it doesn't constrict tree growth or become embedded in the bark.

● Making rubber bands from bicycle inner tubes can also be used to fix boxes. These have the benefit of stretching as the tree grows but over time the rubber may perish and need replacing. You will need to check regularly in case the rubber is gnawed by mice or squirrels.

● Synthetic twine is both elastic and long-lasting (if you avoid using bio-degradable material which may only last a year or so). Again squirrels and mice may chew into the twine, so make regular checks.

Whichever binding option you choose, loop it loosely around the tree trunk to allow the box to sag down about 30 degrees (see diagram above right). Such an arrangement means that as the tree's girth expands you can take advantage of the extra twine length to simply push the box upwards by a few centimetres when required. As native trees are relatively slow growing, you are unlikely to need to do this every year.

BOX FIXING METHODS

1: A wired-on box with a batten fixed to the back wall to ensure it sits clear of rain running down the tree's trunk.
2: Conventional box with overlong back pegged to tree.

POSITIONING YOUR BOX

▲ Left: Taking advantage of a tree that is not completely upright, this correctly positioned box slopes slightly forward to give shelter from the elements.
Right: Eggs and chicks in an upwards-facing box, particularly if it is the open-fronted type, will be exposed to rain and wind.

TOP TIPS FOR DETERRING NESTBOX PREDATORS

Small birds face a daunting array of threats from larger feathered species. The contents of a nestbox are tempting prey for Great Spotted Woodpeckers, Tawny and Little Owls, Carrion Crows, Jays and Magpies. More risk comes in the form of cats, Grey Squirrels, mice and Weasels, so you will need to take active steps to protect eggs and chicks.

Box location

Mounting boxes on walls will present a serious challenge to cats and squirrels, but only if they are out of reach. Keep the box well clear of drainpipes, overhanging eaves, nearby trees or the tops of lower walls as these can all be launchpads for squirrel attacks.

Hanging a box from a wire will help to deter less agile predators such as the domestic moggie, but you will need a cone or other metal barrier fixed above the box to stop a squirrel sliding down in best fireman style!

Placing a box behind prickly plants such as *Berberis*, Holly, *Pyracantha* or *Mahonia* will be a serious deterrent to larger predators, though you will need to protect yourself from the barbs when it comes to cleaning time!

Reduce gripability

Covering the box in a slippery material may be the next line of defence. A covering of plastic, Formica or metal will certainly add to the weather-proofing of your box, though Grey Squirrels will gnaw through the first two if they can get a firm foothold.

Stapling branches of Holly or *Mahonia* onto the roof of the nestbox will deter cats from sitting there, lying in wait for adult or fledgling birds as they come of the entrance hole. Cats are also known to prey on bats, waiting close to a roosting site entrance for them to emerge at dusk. If you have bat boxes, make sure they are remote from branches where cats can lurk.

KEEP THIS ALIEN INVADER AT BAY
Grey Squirrel, a North American species, is a potential pest as far as birds are concerned. Not only will they compete for nuts and grain at birdfeeders, they will gnaw away at birdboxes in the hope of reaching eggs or chicks inside.

PREDATOR PROTECTION
Two effective ways to frustrate
predators reaching vulnerable eggs
or chicks are metal protector plates
for entrance holes (above) or fixing
a baffle inside the nestbox below
the entrance hole (right).

Bring in reinforcement

Grey Squirrels and Great Spotted Woodpeckers often
gain access to eggs and chicks by attacking nestboxes.
To stop these pests enlarging the entrance hole,
choose thicker and harder wood for the front panel.
Alternatively, you can buy metal protection plates to fit
around the entrance hole – these are widely available
via the internet.

In some years when natural invertebrate food is in
short supply, woodpeckers may drill into the front of
wooden nestboxes to take eat chicks. Unfortunately,
having discovered this source of food, woodpeckers may
continue to attack them in later years and you will need
an alternative to wooden boxes.

To thwart woodpeckers some nestbox experts have
had success by sandwiching a layer of rubber between two
pieces of wood to create a bouncy laminated front panel.

The safest commercially available box is made from a
cement and sawdust compound (Woodcrete) and hangs
from a branch or bracket by a wire. Woodcrete is so hard
it will defeat all predators.

Keep it out of reach

Cats may predate nestlings by reaching in through the
entrance hole with their forelimbs, so it is a good idea to
position the hole as high as possible above the floor of
your box. A deep box will also prevent woodpeckers from
taking young when they jump upwards in anticipation of
the parents bringing food.

Deep boxes with high entrance holes are ideal, but
sometimes tits will almost fill a box with nesting material,
so defeating your best efforts to keep them safe.

By fitting a roof with a large overhang, you will be able
to frustrate a cat or squirrel that is sitting on top from
reaching into the box. As a further defence you might like
to fit a shelf (half the width of the box) just under the

OPEN TO ATTACK
Stoats are potential nest
predators in most parts of the
UK and even a wire cage fixed to
such an exposed open-fronted
nestbox as this one would not
stop a determined attack.

entrance hole – with luck nestlings can hide below this when the box is under attack.

It is more difficult to discourage some predators than others. For example, mice, rats and Weasels may all predate the eggs and chicks of nesting birds; their small size and dexterity can make it very difficult to exclude them from your nestboxes. Predation is a natural process and predators often have young of their own to feed.

The smell of success?

Some mammals can be put off approaching areas of the garden by smells they find repugnant, but birds seem immune to this effect. Lay down anti-cat pellets, obtainable from garden centres, around your nest box sites. Some people also have success at deterring pest species such as cats with electronic scarers, which emit unpleasant high frequency sounds when an animal passes through an invisible beam.

Protecting open boxes

Open nestboxes, suitable for Robins or Spotted Flycatchers, are naturally more vulnerable to predators so do your best to place them in well-hidden spots in the garden. As an extra layer of defence you can make a balloon-shaped guard from 40mm chicken wire or other mesh and staple it to the front of the box. The gaps will be too small for larger birds to penetrate, but Weasels will still get through.

The human factor

If you have the opportunity to place nestboxes in public spaces, you will need to think about how to counter human 'predators' such as egg collectors, inquisitive children or mindless hooligans. The best solution is to stain the outside of boxes in brown or green and site the boxes where they will be well concealed – high in trees hidden by leaves or low enough on the trunk to be masked by surrounding scrub layer.

HARD SHELL
SOLUTION
A Great Tit takes food into
a commercially produced
nestbox made from
Woodcrete (a rock-hard
combination of concrete
and sawdust that is
impervious to damage by
predators or weather). The
front panel can be removed
to facilitate cleaning.

CONSTRUCTING YOUR NESTBOX

Your complete guide to the tools, materials and construction
techniques needed to build the most effective nestboxes,
plus some of the pitfalls that you will need to avoid.

WHAT MATERIALS ARE BEST TO USE?

Wood

For anyone considering building their own nestboxes,
then wood is by far the best material to choose, as long
as it is at least 15mm thick. This will prevent the wood
warping and provide sufficient insulation to protect chicks
from heat or cold.

Soft woods, such as pine and cedar, are easy to cut
and their natural resins ensure a long life. Hard woods
such as oak or Beech will also be weather resistent
but may warp when conditions switch from dry to wet.
Buying planed wood or quality plywood is not cheap, so
it may be worth seeing if you can pick up some off-cut
scraps from a timber merchant.

The greener option is to use secondhand timber,
such as old floorboards, skirting boards, packing cases or
pallets, and if you live at the coast it might pay to seek
out suitable pieces of driftwood such as fish boxes or
packing cases. Take care when handling previously used
wood to avoid any sharp nails, screws or staples.

If you do opt for the new wood option, ensure that it
comes from a renewable source: there is no point trying
to improve the habitat for your local birds at the expense
of even more endangered habitats elsewhere.

Manufactured boards

While MDF (medium density fibreboard) has become
a popular material for many DIY projects, it should
not be your first choice for any nestbox that is going
to stand outside. Essentially, MDF consists of sawdust
particles and resin compressed at high temperatures
to form a dense smooth board, but just like chipboard
it has a tendency to absorb water – not a good
trait considering how much rain we get in Britain.
However, if you are planning to put boxes for Swifts or
Starlings into your protected roof space then MDF and
chipboard will do the job nicely.

Marine and exterior grade plywoods will last for
a long time outside, but these materials come with
hefty price tags when bought new.

Metal

We have all grown up used to seeing cute images
of Robins nesting in old kettles, but metal is
probably the least suitable material for you to
consider for a new box. All metals conduct heat very
well, so it is almost impossible to insulate the chicks
from high temperatures. A metal box will also suffer
from excessive condensation, dampening the nest
and its contents.

▲ With careful supervision, making nestboxes is a fun activity which all members of the family can enjoy.

Plastic

Plastics suffer from the same shortcomings as metal – poor levels of insulation lead to overheating in sunlight and low temperatures at night. Condensation inside an all-plastic box is a major problem and even thick plastic will not withstand determined attacks from gnawing squirrels and other rodents.

Large plastic drums, when adapted with large drainage holes and fixed into shady positions, have been successfully adopted by species such as Stock Doves, Jackdaws and Tawny Owls. However, plastic is best avoided when making nestboxes, as are any other materials that might lead to condensation or produce unfavourable environmental conditions within the nestbox. Wood remains the most versatile and useful material for crafting your own nestboxes.

THE TOOLS YOU WILL NEED

Your basic toolkit for making boxes will consist of a handsaw, hammer, screwdriver, a drill (either a power tool or a hand brace) and drill bits. If you plan to use a rubber hinge to attach the roof, then a heavy-duty staple gun is useful. A work bench is a good investment if you plan to carry out more DIY projects because it makes sawing and hole-boring so much easier and safer.

Your carpentry skills may be fairly rudimentary, but don't be deterred from constructing your own boxes from scratch. Remember that in the wild, birds have to take whatever nest opportunities occur naturally, so they won't be judging your woodworking ability too harshly.

If you are a DIY novice and want to avoid spending a lot of money on new drills and other equipment, why not enquire if a neighbour can lend you what you need?

THE ESSENTIALS...

▶ CHISEL, HAMMER AND SCREWDRIVER
Opt for a claw hammer so that you can easily extricate any misplaced or bent nails. Chisel blades need to be kept sharp to be effective so a whetstone is a good investment. Screwdrivers are usually flat-bladed or cross-headed: the latter fit more securely into the screw head.

▲ POWER DRILL
Though it is likely to be your most expensive tool, an electric drill makes cutting entrance holes easy. This one is equipped with a screw-nose centre bit, part of set picked up cheaply at a discount supermarket.

THE TOOLS FOR THE JOB

Woodworking projects, such as making nestboxes for birds and bats or refuges for hibernating hedgehogs, will always be more enjoyable if you have access to good quality tools.

▲ A GOOD QUALITY HANDSAW
Traditional handsaws are all-round woodworking tools equally good for cutting rough timber as well as planed wood. Smaller tenon saws have finer cutting teeth and may be a better option for children to use.

OTHER USEFUL TOOLS...

▲ STAPLE GUN
Heavy-duty staples are a good way to fix rubber hinges to the roof of a nestbox.

▲ WORKBENCH
Workbenches that fold down can be stored without taking up too much space in a shed or garage.

▲ PLIERS
Pliers are useful for removing bent nails and staples, or for cutting and twisting wire.

For those who have a basic toolkit, then you will probably have to lay out money for a set of drill bits to create entrance holes. It is worth keeping an eye out for special offers on multi-size bit kits at discount supermarkets, but if you can only afford one then opt for a 32mm bit as this will potentially allow any of the common small birds to use the box.

An expanding drill bit allows you to cut holes of varying sizes, but they tend to be expensive. You can duck out of drilling any holes by sawing a V-shaped hole directly under the roof of your box. A quick search of the internet will reveal several companies that offer ready-cut nestbox kits and these would appeal to children (working under supervision of course) to assemble with hammer and nails.

CONSTRUCTION METHODS

Having decided you are going to take the DIY option and build your nestbox from scratch, there are several issues to bear in mind to ensure success:

Waterproofing

Rainwater will not only rot wood over time, but waterlogging of the nest could potentially lead to chilling of eggs or even, in extreme cases, nestlings being drowned. So, it is essential to weatherproof your nestbox as much as possible from the very start of its life.

Where possible, ensure the grain of the wood runs vertically down the sides of the box, as this will encourage water to drain rapidly. As an extra waterproofing precaution to prevent rot, you could coat the cut edges of your panels with PVC glue.

When you insert the floor of the box, position slightly above the bottom of the side panels to prevent water collecting on it. If the floor panel fits very tightly to the sides of your box, drill some drainage holes to ensure water can drain out.

If you are using recycled materials such as old pallets,

▲ Make sure the floor of your box sits higher than the bottom of the side panels for maximum protection from rain.

you will probably have to join two or more pieces together to get the required width of panel. To stop water and wind entering the box you will need to cut rebates along each panel edge so that the pieces can be overlapped. Glue these joints for extra security.

Assembling your nestbox

As we have previously discussed you can use nails or screws to fix panels together. Avoid using those made of iron if you live in a particularly wet part of the country as they may rust away long before the box has reached the end of its useful life. If you are using plywood for the box try to avoid screwing or nailing parrallel to the laminations as the layers will probably split.

For extra security you may like to glue the side panels together as well as nailing them, but do not rely on glue alone – over time the wood may flex or shrink and the joint will split apart.

Opening lids or fronts

To make it easier to clean out old nesting material at the end of the breeding season or to inspect the progress of a brood make sure the roof or front panel (your choice) is hinged or fixed in such a way that it can be removed entirely. An opening front panel will probably mean the roof is more waterproof, but draughts may affect the nestlings unless the front panel fits very tightly against the sides.

Boxes with opening fronts need to be opened very carefully to ensure nest contents do not fall out or the young birds fledge prematurely.

Roof options

If you favour a completely removeable roof (a good idea if you are intending to erect many boxes in a woodland and want to speed up the inspection process), then make it big enough to overlap all four sides of the box for maximum weather protection.

It is crucial that squirrels or Pine Martens cannot lift a loose lid, so fix two battens on the underside of the roof to ensure a tight fit against the sides. As a further security measure, drill holes to accommodate loose-fitting nails (see photo on page 41, bottom

right). Alternatively use hooks and eyes to keep the lid secure. If you have staples, you can fashion a roof-lock with three of them and a nail (see photo on page 41, bottom left).

For boxes in gardens a hinged lid is probably the best option: you will have to decide between metal hinges (non-rusting brass ones can be expensive) or a more economical hinge made from rubber. Bicycle inner tubes will do the job nicely, but any hard-wearing flexible synthetic material can be pressed into action. Just be sure it is not so brightly coloured that it makes the nestbox obvious to predators. After a few years rubber may start to perish, so inspect the hinge regularly.

Rubber or plastic hinges can be fixed in place with small tacks or heavy-duty staples. Remember to drill the hole for the box's back plate above the level of the rubber…. if you try to drill through the rubber it will become tangled around the drill bit!

Varying your own design

While the cutting diagrams provided in this guide are based on standard wooden planks, it is easier and cheaper to make boxes from whatever scrap wood is available, so don't feel you have to match measurements

▲ Drive in nails at an angle for more grip.

▲ Buy metal protectors to prevent damage to entrance holes.

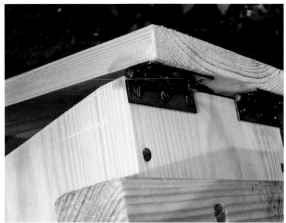

LIFT-UP ROOF OPTIONS
Above: Non-rusting brass hinges means that a larger roof panel can overlap all four sides of the box, thereby giving more protection from rain. Right: A top-opening box with a hinge of rubber cut from an old inner tube.

SECURING THE LID
Bottom left: A simple roof-locking device made from three long staples and a nail. Bottom right: Long nails pass through the box sides to engage the batten and keep the lid secure.

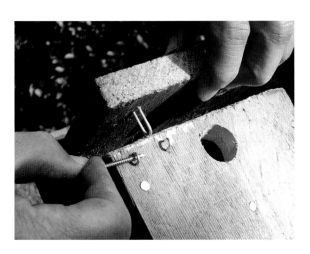

exactly. Apart from the size of the entrance hole, box dimensions are not critical so adapt your plan to the wood available. Just ensure the box is large enough to accommodate your hand so that cleaning our nest material is easy to do.

Unless your wood has weathered outside for some time, it may look very pale when set against a woodland backdrop. This may not be an issue in your own garden, but if you want the box to remain discrete in a woodland or other public space, then consider colouring the outside of the box with water-based stain (green or brown colours are widely available for garden sheds etc). See the next chapter for more information about preservatives.

If you have access to wood which still retains the outer layer of bark, use it for the front panel. Not only does it give a natural appearance, but the extra thickness may help deter squirrels from attacking the entrance hole.

▲ A front panel made from a bark-covered off-cut not only looks more natural but offers extra thickness against squirrel attack.

RUSTIC AND DESIGNER BOXES

There are now plenty of sensible, well-designed ready-made nestboxes on the market, but sadly there are others where a designer has been motivated entirely by appearances rather than the welfare of the bird. Avoid buying any box which is fitted with a perch – most small birds don't need it and it could give a predator a foothold.

OTHER DESIGNS TO AVOID
● Thatched roofs, which will not keep out predators and won't be waterproof for very long.
● Boxes with a feeder tray attached – the traffic of birds coming to feed will create too much disturbance for the parent birds.
● Completely enclosed boxes which cannot be cleaned out at the end of the nesting season.
● Boxes with entrance holes that are too large or too low to give chicks any protection from predators.

PURPOSE-BUILT TILES
Right: Rustic Swift-friendly tiles in Holland, but in the UK more modern varients are available. Above: This is how the Dutch Swift box is accommodated inside the roof space.

Built-in nestboxes

If your property has ramshackle outbuildings, or if you are planning to carry out renovations on your home, there will be an opportunity to incorporate built-in nestboxes for species such as Swift, Starling, Barn Owl and Kestrel. Such boxes, which can be long-lasting and relatively maintenance-free, provide a controlled nesting space compared to untidy, pest-ridden and inaccessible nests built by birds under your eaves.

Before starting work on any new building project, check with specialist building companies which can provide information about special roof tiles with nesting holes for Swifts and building blocks, complete with entrance holes, to replace conventional bricks in a wall.

If your chosen wall is not on public view you could ask the brick-layers to simply leave small gaps, aligned in both inner and outer walls, where you wish to locate nestboxes. Species which nest on ledges or in open holes can simply use the gap left by the missing bricks,

though it would be a good idea to lay a thin strip of wood across the lower front to stop nest material or eggs falling out. Such a site would suit Spotted Flycatchers, Robins, Wrens or Pied Wagtails, depending on the exact location of the hole and the amount of vegetation cover.

If the entrance hole required is smaller than the gap left by the missing brick, fill it with a piece of wood complete with an entrance hole.

Gaps in an old barn or outhouse may already give birds access to the interior, so if that opening is destined to remain unblocked throughout the breeding season it is simply a question of fixing nestboxes in suitable locations inside.

Because the building provides protection from the elements, interior boxes don't need sloping roofs or super-strong wooden panels. An old tea chest or packing crate, for example, will be quite suitable for Jackdaws. Boxes made from chipboard, MDF or even thin plywood will also be OK inside, as long as there is no risk of water damage.

LOOKING AFTER YOUR NESTBOX

Give the nestboxes you place in your back yard long and productive lives with regular maintenance, but also pay attention to improving the garden habitat in which they are located.

NESTBOX CLEANING AND DEALING WITH PARASITES

Many nests, including those in nestboxes, will harbour nest parasites. The main culprits are fleas (*Siphonaptera*), which can occur in large numbers. Their bites can be irritating to humans, so wear gloves whenever handling nest material. It is important to remove old nests because flea larvae will remain and hatch the following year.

Flightless flat-flies (*Hippoboscidae*) occur in large numbers in the nests of Swifts, Swallows and martins. They overwinter in nests as larvae and hatch the following year when the birds return. In nests which have been used regularly over a number of years, flat-fly numbers may actually harm the development of chicks.

Nothing can be done to reduce parasite numbers during the breeding season, but between September 1 and January 31 old bird nests can be removed and the boxes cleaned. Any dead eggs must be destroyed promptly and cannot be kept or sold.

For tits, you can carry out cleaning operations as soon as breeding is over, but bear in mind that other hole-nesting species, including sparrows, may have second or third broods in the same nest. The nests of these species should be left until later in the autumn when it is certain that they are no longer in use.

Don't delay your clean-up for too long in autumn…. if the weather turns cold smaller birds may decide to roost in a nestbox and even build a nest for extra warmth.

When cleaning out nestboxes it is advisable to wear surgical gloves and a dust mask because old nests may harbour fungi growing on damp nest material, which can cause respiratory diseases. To avoid fleas, lice and ticks getting into your house, always carry out the clean-up outside. Old nests can be recycled by depositing them into your compost bin.

A stiff bristled brush, such as an old tooth brush, is a useful tool for removing hardened debris from box corners. To ensure no parasites remain in the empty box, some owners will use a culinary blow-torch to go over all the interior surfaces.

PROVIDING USEFUL NESTING MATERIAL

Building a new nest can be a time-consuming process for parent birds and if they expend too much energy at this stage of the breeding cycle it may eventually lead to them raising fewer chicks.

A completely manicured garden will offer very little in the way of nesting material, so try to leave a few wild patches where the birds can forage for grass or other soft material.

▲ After watching another successful bird breeding season unfold, do not forget to clean out nestboxes ready for next year.

Here's a few other ways you can help:

- Leave patches of moss in your lawn – it remains green throughout the year and for many species it is the most important nest lining material.
- Collect up any feathers you find as these are great for insulating a nest. You may have a neighbour who keeps chickens, or come across a pile of feathers plucked by a Sparrowhawk. To avoid parasites it is best to handle these while wearing gloves, but if you are disposing of an old feather pillow its contents will be pest-free.
- Animal hair is something that birds use naturally, especially if they live close to sheep. The hair of your cat or dog will be equally appreciated so don't throw it in the dustbin when you've had a grooming session.

Long hair, such as that from a horse's mane or tail, should be avoided as it may become caught around adults or developing chicks and result in death or injury.

- Left-over knitting wool is another useful nest material, but to avoid any risk of entanglement, it should be cut into pieces no longer than 5cm.
- Some birds, such as Nuthatches and House Martins, need moist mud for their nest building and in dry summers this can be hard to find. Create a reliable source by sinking an upturned dustbin lid into the ground and fill with a mix of earth, dry grass, water and lime. If you have access to cattle dung, add that to the mixture.
- If you have a pool in the garden, pile mud at the edges and let it slope gently into the water to keep it moist.

COLLECTING NEST MATERIALS
Above: Animal hair this long may entangle the legs of Blue Tit chicks, so cut it into short lengths. Right: Place wool and short hairs into holders for birds to help themselves, or make a mud puddle to attract House Martins.

REPAIRING AND PRESERVING YOUR NESTBOXES

Preserving

Wood that is exposed to the elements needs to be protected. Traditional oil-based preservatives such as creosote should be avoided as the potential toxic risk to birds is not yet fully understood. Happily, there is an abundance of water-based preservatives, normally sold for sheds and fences, on the market.

Amateur artists could use acrylic paint to create special colour or camouflage effects. Even though acrylics and other water-based paints are not toxic, the inside of nestboxes should be left unpainted as plain wood will mimic natural nest holes more closely.

Repairing

Make it a habit to check the soundness of all your boxes before a new breeding season gets underway. Replace any damaged boxes with new ones and then take them away for repair. These will then be the replacement boxes for next season. Small holes caused by wet rot or gnawing squirrels can be covered with a plate made from plywood or metal. You will need a basic repair kit, consisting of hammer, pincers, nails, string and patching material.

You may find that woodpeckers or squirrels have tried to enlarge the entrance hole to get at the nestbox contents. If that is a problem in your area, it is worth considering buying a specially designed metal plate (widely available from garden birdfood suppliers) to guard the entrance.

MAINTENANCE TASKS
You can use a plastic bag to
collect old nest material, but rather
than adding it to landfill, put the
contents into your compost heap.
Right: Re-proof older boxes if they
show any signs of water damage.

TIPS FOR WORKING SAFELY

Making, erecting or cleaning nestboxes are all potentially
hazardous operations and care is definitely needed. Bear in
mind that the long-term interests of birds will not be well
served if you are injured in the process of trying to position
a new box. Here are a few specific points to bear in mind
when getting underway:

● If you are using an unfamiliar tool, check how it should
be used correctly, either by asking a more experienced DIY
enthusiast or viewing demonstrations on internet sites.
● Take care not to use implements, particularly power tools,
for purposes for which they were not intended.
● Do not use power tools to cut or drill into reclaimed
wood as it may contain hidden nails or screws.

● Ensure ladders are secure before you climb them. Check
that thin trees or branches are strong enough to hold the
ladder securely when your weight is added.
● Safety goggles are a good idea when using chisels,
hammering masonry nails into walls or inspecting owl or
raptor boxes. Wildlife photographer Eric Hosking lost an eye
when attacked by an adult Tawny Owl defending its nest.
● Beware electricity, either in the form of an overhead
cable you might touch when carrying a metal ladder, or an
unprotected wire in a shed to which you are nailing a nestbox.

Clearly this cannot be a comprehensive list of all precautions
that should be taken, but common sense is a far better
guide than a book full of detailed rules.

NESTBOXES WITH SMALL ENTRANCE HOLES

THE PERFECT NESTBOX FOR WOODWORKING NOVICES AND PEOPLE WHO ONLY HAVE SMALL GARDENS, THIS DESIGN WILL SUIT THE NEEDS OF A WIDE RANGE OF BIRDS AND CAN BE MADE FROM NEW OR RECYCLED WOOD.

A succesful box needs to have sides and a roof which are water tight, but to avoid any risk of the interior becoming waterlogged it is sensible to drill drainage holes in the floor.

Our diagram (right) shows how you can cut all the components you need to make a box suitable for tits and sparrows from a single plank, but treat the measurements as a guide only. In the wild, birds will make use of any natural spaces they can find and these could be bigger or smaller than our suggested size.

As a rough guide, if you make your box wide enough to accommodate an adult human hand you will find it easy to clean out used nesting material at the end of the breeding season. Building a box that is bigger than our diagram may encourage some birds to lay more eggs, but do not be too ambitious or birds prospecting for a nest site may decide that it is too big and, therefore, unsuitable.

THE ROOF

Make sure your roof panel is long enough to overlap the side containing the entrance hole – this will stop rain dripping inside and may also provide shade from the sun. A piece of wood big enough to overlap all sides of the box is better for weather protection. An angled roof allows rain to run off freely, but a flat-topped box will be fine if it can be fixed to a tree so that the entrance hole is pointing slightly downwards.

It is important that the roof can be removed easily when inspecting the nest or for cleaning the box at the end of the breeding season. See Constructing your Nestbox (pages 36 to 43) for the best options.

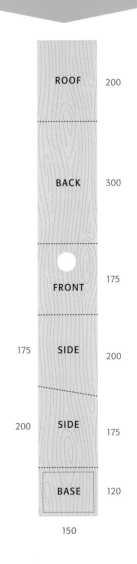

CUTTING TEMPLATE
Rough cut timber
Plank size: 150mm x 1170mm

ROOF   200

BACK   300

FRONT   175

175   SIDE   200

200   SIDE   175

BASE   120

150

WEATHERPROOFING
Weatherproof the roof with water-based preservative and ensure it overlaps the front of the box to stop rain reaching the entrance hole.

ROOF JOINT
To minimise the risk of rain entering the back of the box it is worth cutting a groove into the back plate to accommodate the back edge of the roof.

TOP TIP
A removable roof may help when cleaning a nestbox, but eggs and chicks are potentially at risk from predators unless you take precautions. The best solution is to use a hook-and-eye catch to stop the lid being lifted.

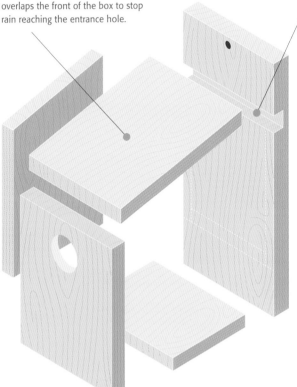

CHOOSING A SIZE FOR THE ENTRANCE HOLE

25mm diameter:
Perfect for Blue, Marsh and Willow Tits.

32mm diameter:
All common small hole-nesting species.

40mm diameter:
The preferred option for Common Redstart.

▶ Use rust-proof nails or screws to join all panels.

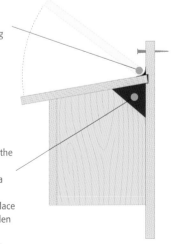

OPENING ROOF
Fit a rubber hinge so that the roof can be lifted easily for cleaning and inspection purposes.

ALTERNATIVE ENTRANCE
An alternative to the traditional round entrance hole is a simple triangular opening. If you place it at the side, widen the roof panel to stop rain entering.

POSITIONING THE ENTRANCE HOLE

Nesting birds tend to prefer a box with the hole in the front panel, rather than the side. A hole on the front is likely to provide a better view for a bird leaving the box, allowing it to more readily spot potential predators. A hole on the side will have a view that is partially obscured by the box and the tree trunk on which it is fixed.

Make sure that the hole is at least 120mm above the floor of the box. A hole lower than this may make it easier for a predator to reach in and take a nestling. Position the hole so that it is sheltered from the elements. Never fix a perch below the hole; birds don't need such a foothold but predators could take advantage.

If you lack the tools to cut a circular hole, why not try a triangular cut in the rear top corner of a side panel?

BLUE TIT
Cyanistes caeruleus

BLUE TITS OCCUPY MANY VARIED NEST SITES. APART FROM NESTBOXES,
THEY WILL USE HOLES IN PIPES, LAMP STANDARDS AND POST BOXES.

16mm

—— 12mm ——

Gardens in all parts of the UK (apart from a few tree-less Scottish islands),
will be visited daily by Blue Tits looking for food. In spring Blue Tits will also
be looking for potential nest site cavities in trees or old walls but they will
readily take to garden nestboxes, too.

A NEST WITH A VIEW

Do not hide the box behind garden plants; Blue Tits like to be able to scan
for predators when leaving a box, so like an unobstructed view. Avoid obvious
sun-traps, such as south-facing walls, to stop chicks overheating. Cold winds
and damp conditions can also cause problems for chicks, so avoid putting
boxes in the shady wind tunnels between houses.

FACT FILE

HOW COMMON:
More than 3.5 million breeding
territories.

WHERE THEY LIVE:
In all parts of the UK where there
are shrubs and broadleaf trees.

NESTBOX TYPE:
Entrance hole of 25mm diameter.

NESTBOX LOCATION:
Site where not threatened by
predators at heights between
1m and 5m above ground.

HOW OFTEN THEY BREED:
Once a year.

NEST MATERIALS:
Moss, lined with feathers and other
soft material.

EGGS:
8–10 white eggs with variable
reddish-brown speckling.

INCUBATION PERIOD:
12–16 days – by female only.

NESTLINGS:
16–22 days before fledging.

CALENDAR	J	F	M	A	M	J	J	A	S	O	N	D
EGG LAYING:												
NESTLINGS:												

WIDESPREAD GARDEN VISITOR

Britain's commonest tit species, the Blue Tit is likely to be observed throughout most habitats in Britain and Ireland, apart from upland areas where trees are few and far between.

TOP TIP
You can tell when breeding begins in April because the female Blue Tit starts carrying moss into the nestbox. Before laying eggs, she will line the nest with feathers and animal hairs.

EARLY STAGES OF LIFE
Top left: When chicks are ready to fledge, the parents may call them from outside the box.
Top right: When Blue Tit chicks hatch they are both blind and featherless.
Left: Females will lay one egg a day, usually in the mornings.

Frustrate domestic cats, which can cause havoc to nesting birds, by placing your nestbox away from any wall-tops or tree branches that would make access easier. Some commercially produced nestboxes feature a perch by the entrance hole; if you've bought such a product, then remove the perch to ensure predators cannot get an easy foothold.

CHOOSE A QUIET SPOT

Parent Blue Tits typically provide nestlings with up to 1,000 food items each day, ideally caterpillars but other insects and spiders may also feature. Birds may be reluctant to approach a box if people are standing right next to it. If you know that the birds are feeding chicks, particularly if these are about a week old when the feeding rate is at its highest, try to avoid spending long periods of time standing near the box. Short visits made to the nest by those monitoring breeding attempts do not impact on breeding success.

DID YOU KNOW?

Hormones produced during the breeding period result in the loss of feathers from the female's abdomen, leading to the formation of a bare patch of skin – known as a 'brood patch'.

This patch becomes wrinkled, swollen and well served by a rich supply of blood. It is the resulting warmth from the brood patch and its blood supply that helps to incubate the eggs.

GREAT TIT
Parus major

THE INCREASED AVAILABILITY OF FOOD AT GARDEN FEEDING STATIONS, COUPLED WITH A RUN OF MILDER WINTERS, MAY HAVE HELPED THIS FAMILIAR SPECIES.

18mm

14mm

Great Tits are regular visitors to gardens in most parts of the country and because they are the biggest of our tit species they tend to dominate feeders and take over nestboxes you may have intended for Blue or Coal Tits. The best way to protect the smaller birds is to provide several boxes with entrance holes restricted to 25mm diameter, which are too small for Great Tits.

In places where nestboxes are not available to them, Great Tits will explore a range of options. Holes, generally wider than 40mm, in trees, stone walls, buildings and rock crevices have all been occupied

FACT FILE

HOW COMMON:
More than 2.5 million breeding territories.

WHERE THEY LIVE:
In all parts of the UK apart from treeless islands and mountainous areas.

NESTBOX TYPE:
Small to medium-sized box with an entrance hole of 28mm diameter.

NESTBOX LOCATION:
Predator-free sites at heights between 1m and 5m above ground.

HOW OFTEN THEY BREED:
Once a year. Second broods uncommon.

NEST MATERIALS:
Twigs or dried roots covered by moss, with a soft lining of hair or other locally available materials.

EGGS:
6–9 white eggs with speckling, mainly at one end.

INCUBATION PERIOD:
12–16 days (average 14 days) – by female only.

NESTLINGS:
15–22 days (average 19 days) before fledging.

CALENDAR	J	F	M	A	M	J	J	A	S	O	N	D
EGG LAYING:												
NESTLINGS:												

SOFT FOODS ARE
FIRST CHOICE
Although adult Great Tits
will feed on sunflower
hearts and other seeds,
they need to find plenty
of caterpillars and other
invertebrates in nearby
trees and garden shrubs
to feed to their ever-
hungry offspring.

◀ In the breeding season, parent birds are in constant action – often, as soon as one bird leaves the nest, the other is waiting to take more food inside. BTO research calculated that the effort required to feed a brood of chicks was equivalent to humans bringing home more than 100kg of shopping every day for three weeks.

successfully and on rare occasions they have managed to raise young in tunnels made by Sand Martins and Kingfishers.

Great Tits generally seek to fill any chamber with nesting material, so it is sensible to limit the size of any box you provide. An unduly large space will commit the adult birds to collecting vast amounts of material, expending energy better saved for when the chicks need feeding.

A base of moss, grass and plant fibre will fill the base of their selected site and the nest of animal hair, wool and other soft material goes on top. Unlike Blue Tits, Great Tits rarely use feathers to line the nest cup.

VARY THE SIZE OF BOXES

While Great Tits will nest successfully in boxes built to our standard cutting diagram, they can appreciate extra space and may raise bigger families in a roomier nestbox. Give them more floor space by making the sides of the box wider (up to 200mm). It has been suggested that Great Tits might prefer the more compact standard nestbox for their winter roosts, so why not try to provide both sizes if your garden is big enough.

Historically, some Great Tits would be evicted from boxes by nesting House Sparrows, but the recent decline in sparrow populations means this happens less often. If you are concerned that there is a risk of this happening, and want to favour Great Tits over House Sparrows, then a possible solution is to build a deeper box (up to 50cm) because it has been suggested that sparrows tend to avoid this design. The other advantage of a deep box is that vulnerable chicks are further from the entrance hole the reach of potential predators.

DID YOU KNOW?

The bill of a Great Tit is longer in the summer than in the winter. Researchers have shown that summer bills are narrower and longer, which makes it easier to grab insects, while winter bills are deeper and shorter so that they can consume beech mast. Their bills wear down during the course of the winter and grow in the spring. There are also differences in bill size between the sexes, with males having chunkier bills, especially during the winter.

MARSH TIT
Poecile palustris

THE MARSH TIT USUALLY NESTS LOW TO THE GROUND, OFTEN USING TREE STUMPS, AND MAY EVEN NEST IN HOLES AT OR BELOW GROUND LEVEL.

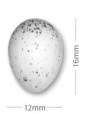

16mm

12mm

Despite its name, the Marsh Tit is a bird that prefers to make its home in broadleaf woodlands, parks or larger gardens. They can also be found in Alder carr and tree-lined streams and rivers, but you will not find them in conifer forests. The ongoing fragmentation of woodlands has played a big part in the Marsh Tit's population decline of more than 50% in 25 years. Damage to the understorey caused by increasing numbers of grazing deer has further reduced the number of suitable nesting territories for a species that shows a distinct preference for nesting close to the ground.

The situation is made worse because Marsh Tits prefer to keep to familiar

FACT FILE

HOW COMMON:
Fewer than 41,000 breeding territories.

WHERE THEY LIVE:
Absent from Ireland, most of Scotland and much of NW England. Favours moist, broad-leaved woodland, orchards, parks and some rural gardens.

NESTBOX TYPE:
Small box, entrance of 25mm diameter.

NESTBOX LOCATION:
Low down, if cats are not a potential danger.

HOW OFTEN THEY BREED:
Once a year.

NEST MATERIALS:
Moss, lined with feathers and other soft material.

EGGS:
7–9 white eggs, with variable speckling.

INCUBATION PERIOD:
13–15 days – by female only.

NESTLINGS:
17–21 days before fledging.

CALENDAR	J	F	M	A	M	J	J	A	S	O	N	D
EGG LAYING:												
NESTLINGS:												

▲ While Marsh Tits will join other species in a feeding party, they drop out as soon as they reach the edge of their territory.

locations and it may take many years for them to discover alternative areas with sufficient nesting holes.

PROVIDE PLENTY OF CHOICE

Marsh Tits are small and may lose out to Great and Blue Tits if you provide only a single box in a woodland site. To avoid this conflict, it is best to erect several boxes for the bigger birds (more than a metre from the ground), plus others for Marsh Tits at almost ground level.

An alternative design, attractive to both Marsh and Coal Tits, can be made from a log of wood. You can find out more about nestboxes made from logs on the next page, together with a photograph of a finished box.

The ongoing fragmentation of woodlands has played a big part in the Marsh Tit's population decline of more than 50% in 25 years.

TOP TIP
The Marsh Tit's distinctive 'pitch-oo' call is the best way to distinguish it from the rarer Willow Tit.

COAL TIT
Periparus ater

IF YOU HAVE MATURE CONIFERS IN YOUR GARDEN, YOU MIGHT BE ABLE TO ATTRACT
COAL TITS, BUT REMEMBER TO PLACE YOUR NESTBOX CLOSE TO THE GROUND.

15mm

12mm

The expansion of commercial conifer forests helped this small tit
species to expand its population in in the 1960s and 1970s and it has
now stabilised at this higher level. Placing boxes in conifer woods will
bring the best results, but a box on an isolated conifer in mixed woodland
is sometimes rewarded too.

Planting conifers in your garden will increase your chances of seeing
Coal Tits and in winters when spruce seeds are in short supply, they can
be attracted to bird feeders.

Coal Tits will nest in standard tit boxes, but prefer those sited low down.
In the wild, Coal Tits seek out cavities on or near to the ground, sometimes
taking over burrows made by mice or voles.

If you or your neighbours have free-roaming cats then chicks will be
at risk, so it will be better to find sites that are well hidden from cats.
If competition from Great or Blue Tits is a problem, simply put up more
boxes with 25mm entrance holes.

ALTERNATIVE HOUSING

An alternative design made from a log is not only
long-lasting, but its more natural appearance is likely
to attract those species, such as Willow Tit, that are
less likely to use a standard box. Log boxes made from
broad-leaf wood tend to rot quite quickly, so it is better
to source a piece of seasoned pine. The natural oils in
conifers act as a preservative, extending the life of your
box. In view of the effort needed to excavate the log's
interior, it is not a job you want to be doing too often!

FACT FILE

HOW COMMON:
More than 760,000 breeding territories.

WHERE THEY LIVE:
Widely distributed across the UK,
usually in coniferous woodland. Highest
densities in Wales, Scotland and Ireland.

NESTBOX TYPE:
Small box, entrance hole of 25mm
diameter.

NESTBOX LOCATION:
Prefers boxes close to the ground, but
will occupy higher ones if there is no
competition from other species.

HOW OFTEN THEY BREED:
Usually once, sometimes twice a year.

NEST MATERIALS:
Moss, lined with hair, fur and wool;
feathers rarely used.

EGGS:
8–10 white eggs, with variable speckling.

INCUBATION PERIOD:
14–16 days – by female only.

NESTLINGS:
18–20 days before fledging.

CALENDAR	J	F	M	A	M	J	J	A	S	O	N	D
EGG LAYING:												
NESTLINGS:												

LOW-DOWN CHOICE FOR COAL TITS

Conifer-loving Coal Tits keep a low profile when selecting natural nest sites or nestboxes. They actively seek out nest sites close to the ground, so they have to be well hidden to escape the notice of predators. Right: Females will bring in fur, hair and other soft materials to line the nest.

HOUSE SPARROW
Passer domesticus

FOLLOWING A DRAMATIC DECLINE IN THE PAST 45 YEARS, THE ONCE-FAMILIAR HOUSE SPARROW NEEDS OUR HELP TO FIND SUITABLE NEST SITES.

22mm

16mm

Why House Sparrow numbers have plummeted from more than 12 million pairs in the 1970s to less than half that today is still not fully understood, but a reduction in the number of available nest sites may be a contributory factor in some areas.

House Sparrows have traditionally exploited gaps in house walls and eaves to build their nests. In more recent times, the house renovation boom has removed many of these niches; providing alternative nesting opportunities through nestboxes may go some way to counter such losses.

In rural areas, House Sparrows will nest close to each other in dense hedgerows or other secure locations and you are more likely to attract them to your garden if you install two or three nestboxes close together (15 to

FACT FILE

HOW COMMON:
Severe decline to 5.3 million breeding pairs. Now red-listed as a bird of conservation concern.

WHERE THEY LIVE:
In all parts of Ireland and the UK, apart from remote parts of Scottish Highlands. Usually associated with human habitation and outbuildings.

NESTBOX TYPE:
Small box, entrance hole of 32mm diameter.

NESTBOX LOCATION:
Above 2m on trees or buildings in undisturbed areas.

HOW OFTEN THEY BREED:
Between one and four times a year.

NEST MATERIALS:
An untidy domed grass nest lined with feathers, hair and wool. Sometimes just a cup when the nest is in a box or small cavity.

EGGS:
4–5 off-white or pale blue eggs, with darker spots.

INCUBATION PERIOD:
11–14 days – by both sexes.

NESTLINGS:
14–15 days before fledging.

CALENDAR	J	F	M	A	M	J	J	A	S	O	N	D
EGG LAYING:												
NESTLINGS:												

KEEPING CLOSE COMPANY
Above: Some people have success with larger multi-chambered House Sparrow nestboxes, but putting individual boxes close together is usually the best option. Left: As chicks get ready to fledge, their constant need for food keeps both parent birds busy.

20cm apart). There are commercially produced boxes which have two or three nesting chambers. Substantial terrace-type boxes that can house a complete colony are also available, but the success of this approach has yet to be properly tested.

Though sparrows seem very comfortable close to people they can be sensitive to disturbance when nesting, so it is a good idea to locate your boxes at least two metres above ground level. Some birds have occupied open-front nestboxes, but they prefer boxes with hole entrances because they offer greater protection from predators.

GOING LARGE

Because House Sparrows build such large untidy nests (up to 30cm in diameter in the wild), they may appreciate boxes that are larger than our standard design. In good breeding seasons when food is plentiful, House Sparrows may attempt to nest up to four times and may add new nest material throughout the season.

After the birds have raised their last family in autumn, they are likely to leave their colonies to forage for grain and weed seeds in nearby scrub or farmland. As with other nesting birds, nestboxes should be cleaned out during the winter months and not earlier.

DID YOU KNOW?

Although adults will feed themselves on wide range of seeds, House Sparrows need to find plenty of aphids and small caterpillars for their growing youngsters, especially in the first few days after hatching.

It is thought that many of the second and third broods being raised in towns fail because there are not enough insects later in the year.

TREE SPARROW
Passer montanus

THOUGH SENSITIVE TO HUMAN DISTURBANCE, TREE SPARROWS ENJOY
BEING PART OF A COLONY, SO PLACE NESTBOXES CLOSE TOGETHER.

19mm

14mm

Despite the fact that some pairs are capable of breeding three times a year, Tree Sparrows have suffered a calamitous UK population crash since the late 1970s. Reductions in the amount of dropped seed in winter stubble is thought to be a major reason for the decline.

Things have started to improve slowly, but we still have only 10% of the numbers present before the 1960s.

Tree Sparrows take readily to nestboxes placed close together, but select your site with care because the birds may be sensitive to disturbance during the early stages of the nesting cycle. If Tree Sparrow is one of your target species, you may find that getting your boxes up during the autumn increases the chances of them being used the following breeding season.

A pair of Tree Sparrows will sometimes finish building their nest several weeks before any eggs are laid, the nest thickly lined with feathers and built on a base of grass, straw and moss. Fresh nesting material may be added during incubation and between successive broods.

At some sites a Tree Sparrow colony may reduce or vanish altogether after three or four years, but a loosely spaced set of other boxes nearby is likely to encourage them to transfer.

A NEST FOR LIFE

Tree Sparrows typically pair for life, and an established pair may remain faithful to the same nest site throughout this time. Both members of the pair share in all activities, from nest construction and incubation, through to brood and feeding the young. Most pairs manage two broods each year, but some have three, leading to a long breeding season, the birds sometimes also using the box for roosting during the winter months.

FACT FILE

HOW COMMON:
UK population declined by 93% between 1970 and 2008. Slow recovery to 200,000 estimated breeding territories today.

WHERE THEY LIVE:
In low-lying areas, generally north of a line between the River Severn and the Wash. Old orchards, suburban parks and gardens, buildings and small woods or copses are favoured.

NESTBOX TYPE:
Small box, entrance hole of 28mm diameter.

NESTBOX LOCATION:
Above 2m on trees in undisturbed areas.

HOW OFTEN THEY BREED:
Two or three times a year.

NEST MATERIALS:
Dry grasses lined with feathers.

EGGS:
5–6 whitish eggs, with brown blotches or speckles.

INCUBATION PERIOD:
11–14 days – by both sexes.

NESTLINGS:
15–20 days before fledging.

CALENDAR	J	F	M	A	M	J	J	A	S	O	N	D
EGG LAYING:												
NESTLINGS:												

TREE SPARROW'S NON-STOP LIFESTYLE

Above: Nestboxes with 28mm wide entrance holes are perfect for Tree Sparrows. Right: Adults will mate in early spring for their first brood, and will still be feeding chicks of the second clutch well into summer. Some pairs may even attempt a third brood if the weather and food supplies are favourable.

PIED FLYCATCHER
Ficedula hypoleuca

LOCATE NESTBOXES IN OPEN WOODLAND GLADES WHERE
PIED FLYCATCHERS CAN FIND PLENTY OF INSECT PREY.

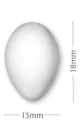

18mm

— 13mm —

Once locally abundant in western and northern Britain, Pied Flycatcher
populations have suffered a marked slump in recent years, leading to
the bird being considered as a species of high conservation concern. The
reasons for this decline are not fully understood, but there is good evidence
that a major problem may be changing conditions on their wintering grounds
in Africa and during migration.

Pied Flycatchers have always been at a disadvantage when it comes to
claiming natural nest sites because they generally do not arrive in Britain
before the middle of April. By that time, Great Tits and other small birds
will already have occupied many tree holes and nestboxes. The situation
has worsened with the increasing numbers of tits leading to increased
competition for nest sites.

FACT FILE

HOW COMMON:
Recently declined to around 19,000
breeding pairs and now red-listed
as a bird of conservation concern.

WHERE THEY LIVE:
Mostly confined to upland woods in
Wales, northern and western England.

NESTBOX TYPE:
Small box with an entrance hole no
bigger than 28mm diameter. Ensure
there is a clear flightpath to entrance.

NESTBOX LOCATION:
Pied Flycatchers are quite happy
using nestboxes positioned at various
heights anywhere within favoured
woodland habitats.

HOW OFTEN THEY BREED:
Once a year.

NEST MATERIALS:
The nest is made of leaves, grass, bark,
moss and lichen and lined with soft
material such as hair, wool and feathers.

EGGS:
6–7 pale blue eggs.

INCUBATION PERIOD:
12–13 days – by female only.

NESTLINGS:
c.16 days before fledging.

CALENDAR	J	F	M	A	M	J	J	A	S	O	N	D
EGG LAYING:												
NESTLINGS:												

FAST-PACED FEEDING REGIME
Male Pied Flycatchers will often bring food to the brown-and-white female when she is incubating eggs. Left: Chicks have to grow quickly, ready to migrate to Africa in late summer.

Pied Flycatchers are very happy to occupy nestboxes if they are located in their preferred habitat of open oak or mixed woodland in upland areas. Ensure there are suitable branches close to the nestbox so that the birds can perch while waiting for insects to fly within range. Woodland with very little ground cover, or open glades, make the best hunting habitats.

AVOID A TAKEOVER

To deter tits taking over a box, erect a small cluster of them at heights between two and four metres off the ground. As tits do not like to nest close to each other, there will always be some boxes left over.

If you don't have the space for a large nestbox scheme, you can block the entrance holes with rags until the Pied Flycatchers make their first appearance.

In order to reduce the numbers of nest parasites present within your Pied Flycatcher nestboxes, consider cleaning out the boxes at the end of the breeding season.

Pied Flycatchers have always been at a disadvantage when it comes to claiming natural nest sites because they generally do not arrive in Britain before the middle of April.

NUTHATCH
Sitta europaea

IF A NUTHATCH MANAGES TO RAISE A FAMILY IN A NESTBOX,
IT IS LIKELY TO USE IT AGAIN IN SUCCESSIVE YEARS

19mm

14mm

The Nuthatch is one of our most distinctive looking birds, but it can sometimes be hard to spot as it forages for food on the trunks and branches of mature trees. It is the only UK species which regularly descends a tree trunk head first as it looks for beetles and spiders on the bark.

The British population has been increasing steadily in recent years, and even though adult birds are very reluctant to leave their established territories, young birds are expanding into areas such as southern Scotland (first recorded in the Borders in 1989).

▲ Hungry chicks react with open beaks when they hear an adult Nuthatch approaching the nestbox with food.

Nuthatches use natural tree holes of varying sizes for their nesting attempts and are quite happy to use nestboxes, which they will adapt by plastering mud around the entrance hole. By controlling the size of the entrance hole, nuthatches can reduce the risk of the nesting attempt being lost to a nest predator.

The adults will also plaster under the lid to fill any gaps, so care is needed to make sure dried mud doesn't fall into the nest if you wish to inspect inside the box.

FACT FILE

HOW COMMON:
More than 200,000 breeding territories.

WHERE THEY LIVE:
Common in woodland habitats in England and Wales, but absent in the Fens, East Yorkshire and most of Scotland.

NESTBOX TYPE:
Small to medium-sized box with an entrance hole of 32mm diameter.

NESTBOX LOCATION:
Between two and three metres above ground.

HOW OFTEN THEY BREED:
Once a year.

NEST MATERIALS:
The floor of nestboxes or natural cavities are covered in wood chips and leaves.

EGGS:
6–8 white eggs with variable red speckling.

INCUBATION PERIOD:
15–16 days – by female only.

NESTLINGS:
23–25 days before fledging.

CALENDAR	J	F	M	A	M	J	J	A	S	O	N	D
EGG LAYING:												
NESTLINGS:												

WELL-NAMED MASTER OF WOODLAND

The Nuthatch, which gets its name from its habit of wedging acorns, nuts or seeds into a crevice before hammering them open with its powerful bill, customises nestboxes by plastering mud under the roof and sometimes around the entrance hole.

REDSTART
Phoenicurus phoenicurus

NESTBOXES CAN MAKE ALL THE DIFFERENCE FOR LATE-ARRIVING
MIGRANT REDSTARTS WHICH MISS OUT ON NATURAL NEST HOLES.

19mm

14mm

FACT FILE

HOW COMMON:
Around 100,000 breeding territories.

WHERE THEY LIVE:
Common in Wales and northern
England. Also in SW England, but largely
absent from East Anglia, the Midlands,
Ireland and much of Scotland.

NESTBOX TYPE:
A variety of different small to
medium-sized boxes with 40mm
diameter square or circular holes.

NESTBOX LOCATION:
Between one and three metres
above ground.

HOW OFTEN THEY BREED:
Once or twice a year.

NEST MATERIALS:
Dead grass, bark, moss and roots,
lined with feathers and animal hair.

EGGS:
6–7 pale blue eggs.

INCUBATION PERIOD:
12–14 days – by female only.

NESTLINGS:
14–15 days before fledging.

A recent increase in our breeding Redstart population has brought
numbers back to the levels they were at during the late 1960s, when
monitoring first began. Warmer weather appears to have led to earlier
nesting and improved breeding success, but the species has still to
recolonise many former haunts.

These migrants arrive in the UK in early April and, like Pied Flycatchers,
they face stiff competition from native species when it comes to finding
good nest sites. When holes in trees, walls or rocks have already been taken,

CALENDAR	J	F	M	A	M	J	J	A	S	O	N	D
EGG LAYING:												
NESTLINGS:												

▲ Male Redstarts will forage for insects and berries in foliage, but are just as likely to take insect prey in flight, launching itself from a favoured perch.

Redstarts have been known to nest under brushwood or amid tree roots.

Redstarts are most commonly found near oak woodland or parkland with scattered trees and are happy to occupy nestboxes if they meet their own design preferences!

Birds in different areas seem to have a liking for particular box designs (see diagram of alternatives that have proved popular), so it may pay to do a bit of research about the locally preferred design before starting work.

KEEPING THEM IN THE DARK

The common feature of these boxes is that they are larger than standard tit boxes, with larger entrance holes, but darker nesting chambers. Placing the box in a shady spot will help control light levels, as will placing the entrance hole in a corner of the front panel. Though some Redstarts will adopt an open-fronted box you can increase their chances of success by fitting a partition across part of the box floor to create a darker area underneath.

Site your box between one and three metres above the ground, preferably on an oak tree – either in a large garden or close to a woodland edge. Ensure there are plenty of song posts nearby to help males defend their chosen territory. Male Redstarts also indulge in beautiful display flights and will often fly-catch from a favoured perch, providing opportunities for you to view these stunning birds.

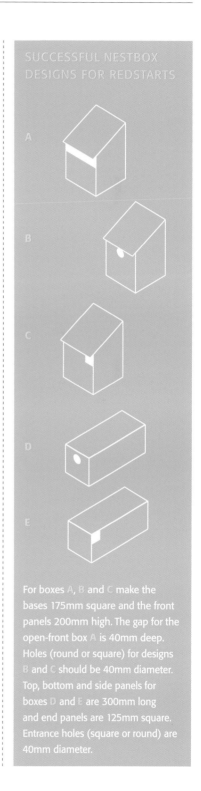

SUCCESSFUL NESTBOX DESIGNS FOR REDSTARTS

A

B

C

D

E

For boxes A, B and C make the bases 175mm square and the front panels 200mm high. The gap for the open-front box A is 40mm deep. Holes (round or square) for designs B and C should be 40mm diameter. Top, bottom and side panels for boxes D and E are 300mm long and end panels are 125mm square. Entrance holes (square or round) are 40mm diameter.

NESTBOXES WITH MEDIUM-SIZED ENTRANCE HOLES

THIS TYPE OF BOX IS NOT ONLY BIGGER BUT HEAVIER THAN THE SMALL-HOLE NESTBOX, SO MORE CARE WILL BE NEEDED TO FIX IT SECURELY, BOTH FOR YOUR OWN SAFETY BUT ALSO TO KEEP THE BOX AND CONTENTS INTACT.

MATERIALS AND CUTTING DIAGRAM

The cutting diagram gives dimensions for a typical medium box made from a single plank of rough cut timber. A lighter alternative is exterior quality plywood; because you can buy this in the form of a large sheet you can cut it to specific sizes of your own choosing.

If you opt for a rough cut plank, do not skimp when it comes to materials. Make sure the nails or screws that you use to construct the box are substantial enough to accommodate the extra weight over a long period of time. Ensure the box is firmly attached to a tree trunk or building with two screws at the top of the back plate and one or two at the bottom.

DRAINAGE

An entrance hole of 45mm diameter risks letting in rain, so drainage is important in larger boxes. If your woodworking skills are not top notch you might find that the base of the box does not fit precisely inside the walls, but do not rely on these gaps for drainage. As wood gets wet it will swell, so it is best to drill a number of holes in the base as an insurance policy.

VARYING THE SHAPE OF ENTRANCE HOLES

While the traditional circular entrance hole is aesthetically pleasing to us, it is irrelevant to a bird; in the wild a bird will make use of any shaped crevice or hole it finds in a suitable habitat. This is good news if you want to avoid the expense of buying a large twist bit for your drill or the effort of using a fine-toothed fretsaw to make a circular hole.

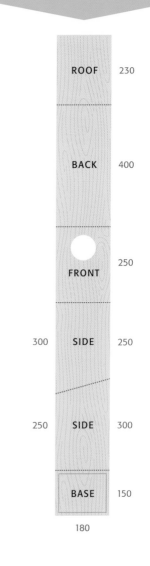

CUTTING TEMPLATE
Rough cut timber
Plank size: 180mm x 1580mm

ROOF — 230
BACK — 400
FRONT — 250
SIDE 300 — 250
SIDE 250 — 300
BASE — 150
180

ALTERNATIVE ENTRANCE HOLE SHAPES

45cm square and triangular holes are acceptable alternatives if you don't have a power drill and hole-boring bit to make the circular entrance.

Square entrance hole.

Triangular entrance hole.

▶ Use rust-proof nails or screws to join all panels.

BACK PLATE HOLES

Remember to drill holes in the back plate before you affix the rubber hinge, otherwise it will snag the drill bit.

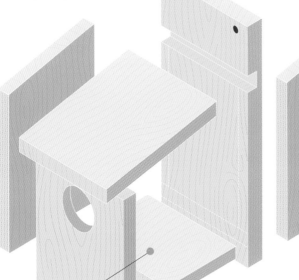

ATTRACTING WOODPECKERS

For most bird species it is not a good idea to put nesting material inside a new box, but if you hope to attract a Great Spotted Woodpecker the opposite is true.

This woodpecker will not occupy any space is has not excavated for itself, so you will need to stuff your newly-created box with natural material such as Birch taken from a dead, fallen tree. This needs to be soft enough to be sliced with a knife in order to fit snugly inside the box.

DRAINAGE HOLES

To avoid the risk of flooding, drill several holes into the floor of the box.

TOP TIP
Though boxes made from exterior-grade plywood are lighter than those using sawn timber, they are more expensive, so check local salvage yards.

The simplest alternative is to cut a triangle shape from the top of the front wall: make each side around 50mm in length. A 45mm square is another option, but will take more effort because cutting the bottom line is not straightforward. Use a drill to make a series of holes just above the cut line and then use hammer and chisel to remove the wood between the holes. The finished line will be ragged but can be cleaned up with sandpaper.

OTHER SPECIES

Though these boxes are not intended for smaller species, it is perfectly possible that a pair of Great Tits might move in if other nest sites are not available.

STARLING
Sturnus vulgaris

STARLING POPULATION LEVELS HAVE DROPPED ALARMINGLY
IN RECENT DECADES, BUT NESTBOXES CAN HELP.

30mm

21mm

Though Starlings are still seen regularly in many parts of Britain, their overall population is less than half what it was in the 1970s. Reasons for the decline are not fully understood, but changes in farming practice - such as the loss of permanent pasture - may have reduced the amount of invertebrate food items on which they depend.

There is good evidence that changes in overwinter survival rates of young birds are driving to the decline, but other factors may also be contributing. Providing nestboxes may be helpful, and the monitoring of these can certainly contribute much-needed knowledge.

Starlings are naturally gregarious, so will happily nest in close proximity to their neighbours. That means you can group several boxes high (above 2.5 metres) on a house wall or, if you have a big enough garden, on adjacent trees. On the latter, make sure that flight paths to the boxes are not blocked by surrounding vegetation.

A HEAD FOR HEIGHTS

Before house renovation became so fashionable, Starlings would often take advantage of gaps in eaves to enter loft spaces to build their nests. With this in mind, even if you live in a high-rise building you could attract Starlings to boxes positioned over your balcony.

If you live in an older property where Starlings are nesting in your roof space you will have to live with these noisy neighbours until breeding is clearly over. The peak period for nesting is in May and if the birds are successful you will see the fledged youngsters begging for food in the garden. Many Starling pairs will go on to make a second nesting attempt once the chicks from the first have fledged.

CALENDAR	J	F	M	A	M	J	J	A	S	O	N	D
EGG LAYING:												
NESTLINGS:												

FACT FILE

HOW COMMON:
More than 1.7 million breeding birds in Britain and up to 500,000 in Ireland. Starling numbers have fallen by 89% in Britain since the mid-1970s. Now red-listed as a bird of high conservation concern.

WHERE THEY LIVE:
In all parts of the UK apart from remote mountainous areas in central Wales and NW Scotland. Often nests in or close to human settlements.

NESTBOX TYPE:
Medium-sized box with circular entrance hole of 45mm diameter. Triangular or square entrance holes also possible.

NESTBOX LOCATION:
Site at heights above 2.5m with direct clear flight-path.

HOW OFTEN THEY BREED:
One, sometimes two attempts per year.

NEST MATERIALS:
A heap of plant material, lined with feathers, wool and moss. In long-used traditional sites, the nest may be several layers deep.

EGGS:
4–5 pale blue eggs, but sometimes up to nine.

INCUBATION PERIOD:
11–15 days – by both sexes, but with female doing most of the work.

NESTLINGS:
17–22 days before fledging.

ALL CHANGE FOR THE BREEDING SEASON

In good light the Starling's green and purple metallic-looking plumage is eye-catching, but there is a distinct difference between its winter garb (spotted) and the much plainer look they adopt for the breeding season.

CHORAL ATTRACTION
Left: A male Starling will sing enthusiastically to attract a female – but he will not necessarily be a faithful partner.
Above: The female will complete the nest before laying between four and seven eggs.

The male begins the breeding cycle by building the base of a nest from dry grass and leaves and then advertises its availability by singing to females from close to the nest entrance. The female completes the nest by making a nest cup and lining it with fine grasses, moss and feathers.

HERBAL REMEDIES?

Studies in Europe have shown that male Starlings will collect a wide range of herbs and other plants to add to the nest before laying. Volatile compounds in the plants were thought to reduce the number of parasites but that theory has been discounted. Instead it appears they stimulate elements in the immune system of the young birds to help them cope better with the harmful effects of mites and fleas etc.

Most Starling clutches contain four or five eggs and are laid in early April. Pairs breeding within a single colony may show a high degree of synchrony in terms of the when the first eggs are laid. Successful pairs will usually attempt a second brood in the same box without adding much new material to the nest. Successful boxes will be in demand year after year, so be sure to thoroughly clean the box during winter to reduce a build-up of parasites.

DID YOU KNOW?

Some male Starlings are less than faithful husbands. While those that remain with one partner will generally help produce a second clutch, some individuals that mate with several females can be responsible for up to six clutches in a single breeding season.

Starlings may also indulge in egg-dumping, where a female will lay one of her eggs in the nest of another bird. It is thought that it is this practice that can sometimes lead to the presence of Starling eggs on the ground near a nestbox or natural nest cavity.

GREAT SPOTTED WOODPECKER
Dendrocopos major

AN EXPANDING POPULATION MEANS THAT GREAT SPOTTED
WOODPECKERS MAY MAKE GREATER USE OF NESTBOXES IN FUTURE.

26mm

19mm

As Britain's commonest woodpecker is well equipped to excavate its
own nest chamber from any soft-wooded deciduous tree, this species is
not a frequent occupier of nestboxes. However, as its population continues
to expand, a lack of natural nesting areas may encourage more of them to
move into spare garden territories, if they are large enough.

This species' population increased rapidly in the 1970s at a time when
Dutch Elm Disease greatly boosted the amount of standing dead timber and
its associated insect life. The ecological factors underlying a second surge
in woodpecker numbers in the 1990s are not yet fully understood, but the

FACT FILE

HOW COMMON:
An expanding population of up to
140,000 pairs in the UK.

WHERE THEY LIVE:
A recent arrival in Ireland, Great Spotted
Woodpeckers are found in most part of
England and Wales, plus wooded areas
in Scotland. Mixed and broad-leaved
woodland is preferred.

NESTBOX TYPE:
Medium-sized box with circular entrance
hole of 50mm diameter. Triangular or
square entrance holes also suitable.

NESTBOX LOCATION:
Fix to trees at heights between three
and five metres.

HOW OFTEN THEY BREED:
Once a year.

NEST MATERIALS:
No soft material is added once a hole
has been excavated in a tree.

EGGS:
5–6 white eggs.

INCUBATION PERIOD:
10–13 days – by both sexes, with males
tending to favour the night shift.

NESTLINGS:
20–24 days before fledging.

CALENDAR	J	F	M	A	M	J	J	A	S	O	N	D
EGG LAYING:				▓	▓							
NESTLINGS:					▓	▓						

FEMALES ARE NEVER REDHEADS

While a male Great Spotted Woodpecker has a patch of red on the back of its head, the female does not. Both sexes show the deep red plumage under the tail.

JOINT EFFORTS
Both sexes will excavate material from nestboxes before occupying it. They also spend about 10 days teaching red-headed fledglings how to find food.

species may be benefiting from the maturation of new forests and from the increasing provision of winter food in gardens.

Another factor may be linked to the decline in Starling numbers. A long-term study in southern England showed a connection between improved breeding success in Great Spotted Woodpeckers and a decrease in nest site interference by similar-sized Starlings.

FILLING THE VOID

Most bird species that are happy to use a nestbox do not excavate their own nest holes in the wild, but of course that is not the case for Great Spotted Woodpeckers. If you are to succeed in attracting them to take over a nestbox, you need to replicate nature and give them material they can remove before nesting.

Stuff a medium-sized box with loose material such as the rotten or soft wood that occurs in the wild. Fill the box except for a small indentation behind the entrance hole. This simulates a natural wound in a tree trunk – a guaranteed weak spot where hole boring will be easier to start.

Seek out a secluded tree with an unobstructed flight path to host the box, which should be sited at least three metres off the ground.

DID YOU KNOW?

A male woodpecker seeking to attract a mate will often drum on hard surfaces (metal posts as well as trees) for up to 600 times a day, and even when he has paired up he will defend his territory with up to 200 drumming sessions. Females also drum to stay in contact, but much less frequently.

To cushion the bird's brain it is equipped with shock absorbant tissue between the base of the bill and the skull.

NESTBOXES WITH LARGE ENTRANCE HOLES

WHEN IT COMES TO LARGE NESTBOXES, YOUR MOTTO SHOULD BE 'TAKE CARE'. ENSURE IT IS MADE STRONG ENOUGH TO WITHSTAND HARSH WEATHER AND ALWAYS HAVE PLENTY OF ASSISTANCE WHEN IT COMES TO LIFTING AND FIXING THE BOX IN PLACE.

CORE MATERIALS

Large boxes made from rough sawn timber are generally too heavy to be easily positioned and require very strong mounting arrangements. New planks of wood are likely to be expensive too. An effective alternative is exterior-quality plywood, sometimes called marine ply. While it can be bought new in large sheets it is not cheap, so look for old pieces that have been discarded.

When using plywood, it will be necessary to fit 25mm square battens at all junction points to ensure that there is something solid to hold nails or screws. To stop rain seepage, it is a good idea to coat all cut plywood edges with PVA glue to make a waterproof seal.

ALTERNATIVE MATERIALS

Any wooden container, such as a barrel or packing crate of the required size, can be pressed into service as a nestbox, but you may need to cover these with roofing felt to ensure they are completely waterproof. Hardboard, chipboard or thin sheets of plywood will rot quickly if exposed to water, so only use these materials for boxes located inside buildings.

LOCATION

Large boxes can be very obvious, so avoid siting them where they could be targeted by vandals or inquisitive children. In rural settings you might be able to colour the exterior of the box to blend in with the background vegetation, while in urban areas the best policy is to site boxes high on buildings – if it is safe to do so.

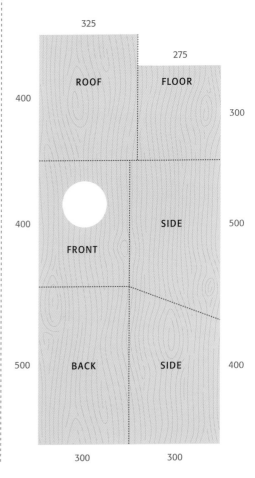

CUTTING TEMPLATE
12mm exterior grade plywood
Sheet size: 600mm x 1300mm

Diameter of entrance hole
(round or square) is 150mm

325

ROOF

400

275

FLOOR

300

400

FRONT

SIDE

500

500

BACK

SIDE

400

300

300

INTRODUCING A PERCH TO LARGE NESTBOXES

Some species such as Tawny Owl will appreciate having a perch incorporated into your nestbox design. Ideally, this will be made of strong dowelling wood and situated towards the front of one of the side walls.

In this position, it can be easily reached by fledgling birds, which need to stretch their wings, but are not yet ready to fly. Adults will also fly into the perch before entering the box with food for the youngsters.

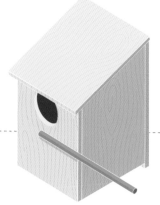

EXTRA SECURITY
All joints need to be reinforced with wooden battens so that screws or nails can be fixed securely.

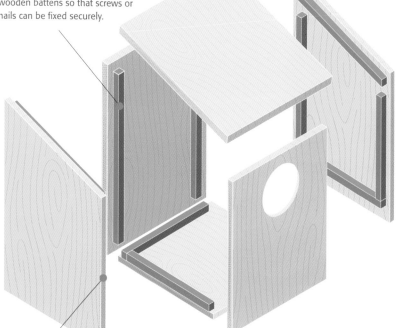

PREPARING THE NEST

Birds that use large nestboxes prefer them to have a layer of loose dry material over the floor. Shredded bark from a garden centre is ideal, though you can create your own version by passing twigs and branches through a shredder. Wood shavings are another alternative, but avoid peat or other soft materials because they will retain moisture and heat up as they decompose.

WATERPROOFING
Before assembling the box, coat all plywood edges with PVA glue to provide extra waterproofing.

TOP TIP
When fixing a large box onto a tree, use a rope over a nearby branch to lift it to the required height – never attempt to carry it up the ladder.

▶ Fix rust-proof nails or screws into wooden battens previously glued into position.

ENTRANCE
As a circular hole of 150mm or more is larger than can be cut by conventional wood-boring equipment, you will need to accomplish the task with a jigsaw. However, an easier option is to cut a square entrance hole out of the front panel.

DRAINAGE
Potentially, rain is likely to enter boxes through large entrance holes, so it is important to drill drainage holes into the floor of your box. For the box size shown in the diagram, drill up to 10 5mm holes. Another good tip is to seat the floor slightly above the bottom of the side panels to prevent water seepage.

JACKDAW
Corvus monedula

THE SMALLEST MEMBER OF THE CROW FAMILY IS AN INTELLIGENT
SPECIES WITH AN EXPANDING POPULATION IN BRITAIN.

36mm

25mm

Though Jackdaws commonly feed in farmland and will occupy a variety
of nesting sites, including deep inside old trees, derelict ruins, quarries and
sea cliffs, they are more than happy to nest in urban areas.

However, if you live in a town or large village, give some careful
consideration to the feelings of your neighbours before trying to tempt
this species. As a gregarious, communal-nesting species, Jackdaws are very
vocal so your neighbours might not appreciate having the smallest member
of the UK crow family at close quarters.

FACT FILE

HOW COMMON:
A stable population of around
1.3 million pairs.

WHERE THEY LIVE:
Throughout the British Isles, apart
from areas of western Scotland and
western Ireland. Favours open country,
woodland edge and larger gardens.

NESTBOX TYPE:
Large box with a large entry hole
of at least 150mm diameter.

NESTBOX LOCATION:
Fix to trees or buildings above three
metres. Clear flightpath essential.

HOW OFTEN THEY BREED:
Once a year.

NEST MATERIALS:
Sticks lined with wool, animal hair,
moss and other soft materials. In smaller
natural holes there may be no twigs.

EGGS:
4–5 pale blue eggs,
with some darker speckles.

INCUBATION PERIOD:
21–22 days – by female only.

NESTLINGS:
22–28 days before fledging.

CALENDAR	J	F	M	A	M	J	J	A	S	O	N	D
EGG LAYING:												
NESTLINGS:												

ADAPTABILITY THE KEY TO SUCCESS

The Jackdaw's wide-ranging choice of food items and its ability to nest in very diverse locations means it is well equipped to thrive, when other more specialist species might falter.

NEST CONSTRUCTION
Male and female Jackdaws, which pair for
life, will collect sticks and a wide range of
other materials to make very large nests.
Right: Inside a very messy nestbox after
the family of fledglings has departed.

Although Jackdaws will breed successfully in an isolated nestbox, they are
colonial birds and so will also benefit from having several suitable nest sites,
or boxes, available within a small area. There is a long history of Jackdaws
nesting in building cavities – think how they take to chimneys – so they will
readily adopt a nestbox that has been built into a loft space with an entrance
through a gable end.

Jackdaws will often nest quite high, and one pair was recorded in a nest
situated 70 metres above the ground in a tower. However, you do not need
to go to those extremes with your Jackdaw boxes. Any location above three
metres high, that offers a clear flight path and isn't too exposed, is likely to
meet with approval.

STANDARD SIZE BOXES THE BEST OPTION

Building your box bigger than the suggested measurements is likely to cause
extra work for the occupants. The adult birds will continue to add twigs to their
nest until it reaches the desired height and if you make the box too big, they
may end up adding a lot of unnecessary material.

Nesting material will be added each year if a pair of Jackdaws finds a site
that meets all their needs. More than one nest on record consisted of a heap
of twigs three metres deep. A nest of this size built inside a still-used chimney
will inevitably cause problems, so make sure you have wire guards fitted to
stop the birds gaining access.

DID YOU KNOW?

The Jackdaw's recent population
growth can be partly attributed to
its varied diet, which means food
shortages are rare. They mainly
eat seeds, fruit and invertebrates
but they will also peck at road
kill or take other birds' eggs.

Their diet varies depending
on their location, so insects
are important near farms, but
in urban and woodland areas
seeds and fruit make up more
of the diet.

STOCK DOVE
Columba oenas

STOCK DOVES MAY ATTEMPT TO BREED UP TO FOUR TIMES
A YEAR, SO DO NOT CLEAN BOXES TOO EARLY.

38mm
29mm

For the past 50 plus years, populations of Stock Dove in the UK have been recovering after a serious slump caused by the over-use of organochlorine seed dressings on farmland, which affected their breeding productivity. This smaller cousin of the Wood Pigeon is amber-listed as a species of conservation concern because the UK population is of global importance.

The word 'stock' in the common name of this species comes from the Old English 'stocc' meaning 'stump, post or tree trunk' and reflects that in the wild this is one of only two pigeon species in Britain to nest in tree holes or other natural cavities. For that reason, Stock Doves are very happy to use nestboxes, especially where mature woodland is in short supply.

FACT FILE

HOW COMMON:
Thought to be around 260,000 breeding territories.

WHERE THEY LIVE:
A resident species most abundant in lowland England, but absent in much of NW Scotland, western Wales and Ireland.

NESTBOX TYPE:
Large box with a large entry hole of at least 150mm diameter.

NESTBOX LOCATION:
Fix, at a height above three metres, to trees or buildings overlooking open fields.

HOW OFTEN THEY BREED:
Usually 2-3 broods a year.

NEST MATERIALS:
Sticks and roots, lined with wool, animal hair, moss and other soft materials. Multiple broods create a deep layer of droppings in the course of a breeding season.

EGGS:
Usually two creamy white eggs, sometimes just one.

INCUBATION PERIOD:
16–18 days – by both sexes.

NESTLINGS:
27–28 days before fledging.

CALENDAR	J	F	M	A	M	J	J	A	S	O	N	D
EGG LAYING:												
NESTLINGS:												

RAPID CHICK GROWTH
It takes only four weeks for newly-hatched chicks (above) to grow strong enough to leave the nest. Left: Stock Doves will occupy boxes inside buildings, though outdoor locations near feeding areas are generally preferred.

The best sites for nestboxes are those close to or overlooking open fields where they can feed. It is important the doves have clear flightpaths to the box and they will appreciate it if you add a landing platform near the entrance hole.

NEST FAILURES

Stock Doves seem to suffer from high levels of nest failure, with chick and egg losses resulting from nest predation or the loss of parent birds. Losing one clutch is not a disaster for these birds, considering their productivity. Two or three clutches a year is normal, four is not exceptional and one pair were recorded to have raised five broods.

Sometimes eggs are laid in nests still occupied by the chicks of the previous attempt, and it is possible their droppings will foul the eggs, preventing them from hatching. If you erect two nestboxes on adjacent trees, a pair can start laying eggs in the other box while still raising fledglings in the first.

Despite the mess left in each box, do not clean it out until the end of the year; Stock Doves can nest into late October or even November in some cases. Once clean, line the box with fresh bark or wood shavings. As a reward for your efforts, you can enrich your compost heap with the old nest contents.

DID YOU KNOW?

Stock Doves have been recorded nesting in cavities in buildings, crevices in sea cliffs and even in Rabbit holes in areas where trees are in short supply. In the past, East Anglian warreners (Rabbit farmers) would identify holes being used as Stock Dove nest sites and place crossed-sticks across the entrance. It meant the parents could continue to feed the chicks while preventing them from leaving the nest, so they could be taken later for the pot.

TAWNY OWL
Strix aluco

THOUGH THEY PREFER TO NEST IN MATURE BROADLEAF WOODLANDS,
TAWNY OWLS COMMONLY VISIT GARDENS TO HUNT OR ROOST.

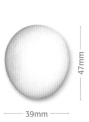

47mm

39mm

Ideally, a nestbox for a Tawny Owl will be deeper than our standard design (up to 800mm in length) to give the chicks plenty of growing room. The young birds have a habit of leaving the nest before they can fly freely and spend several days scrambling about in nearby branches. Fixing a sturdy perching pole or platform alongside the entrance hole will assist the young birds in their first explorations.

If you find an immature bird, apparently helpless, at ground level, don't rush to take it to a rescue centre. The adults will continue to feed the youngster until it can fly, so just place it as high as you can manage into vegetation to escape the attention of dogs, cats and children.

FACT FILE

HOW COMMON:
A resident species numbering around 50,000 pairs. Now amber-listed as a bird of conservation concern because of a recent decline in numbers.

WHERE THEY LIVE:
Widespread in mainland UK, but absent from Ireland and many islands. Favours woodland of all types, and larger wooded gardens.

NESTBOX TYPE:
Large box with a large entry hole of at least 150mm diameter.

NESTBOX LOCATION:
Fix at a height above three metres, to trees offering a clear flightpath to the box.

HOW OFTEN THEY BREED:
Once a year.

NEST MATERIALS:
No material added to nest hole, but will make a scrape in any existing debris.

EGGS:
2–3 white eggs, sometimes up to five.

INCUBATION PERIOD:
28–30 days – by female.

NESTLINGS:
32–37 days before fledging.

CALENDAR	J	F	M	A	M	J	J	A	S	O	N	D
EGG LAYING:												
NESTLINGS:												

SITTING PRETTY
Left: A sturdy tree branch fixed to an upright box makes a rustic perch for this adult Tawny Owl. Inside the box there may be up to five eggs laid but generally only two or three chicks will survive to fledging.

NESTBOX LOCATION

Locate your nestbox on a mature tree within woodland. Nailing or strapping the box in an upright position is the easiest option, but in some areas the owls seem to prefer boxes that are slung at an angle with the entrance hole in the roof. Strapping this type of box beneath a large side branch is not easy, even with several friends to help, so a better option is to nail sturdy battens to the tree trunk and fix the box at an angle on these.

Half-grown Tawny owlets, which have not yet developed their flight feathers, seem keen to explore the world beyond their nestbox and will indulge in a phase called 'branching', when they climb and flutter around in trees at night. The adults locate them by their contact calls and will provide food until they fly.

Some owlets will spend time on the ground during this phase, but are adept at climbing back into trees again. Adult owls will continue to feed the youngster until it can fly, so just place it as high into vegetation as you can manage to help it escape the attention of dogs, cats and children. Always wear strong gloves to handle the chick – its talons are sharp and its grip is fierce.

It may help the owls to move up and down if you glue pieces of wood to the smooth sides of the box to give more grip.

TOP TIP
Be aware, Tawny Owls have sharp talons and a fearsome reputation for defending their chicks!

▲ Chimney-style boxes are open to the elements, so need to be angled away from prevailing rain and wind.

In remote, undisturbed areas you can position the nestbox as low as three metres above the ground, but in more populated areas a height of four metres or more may be required to ensure the owls are not disturbed by people. To avoid the large entrance hole (at least 150mm diameter, but up to 200mm is okay) admitting too much rain or wind, face the box entrance away from the prevailing weather conditions.

Tawny Owls breed early in the year, so nestboxes need to be in place by December at the latest. Visit likely territories at this time of year to listen for the owls – they are particularly vocal in the run-up to breeding.

Bear in mind this species has a fearsome reputation for defending its chicks with its razor-sharp talons, so on no account approach the nest in the breeding season. Bird ringers will wear crash helmets and safety goggles when ringing the chicks.

When cleaning the boxes after the young birds have fledged, it is worth examining prey remains to record what animals have been eaten and sometimes to recover bird rings. Any rings found should be reported to BTO (see page 148 for more details).

DID YOU KNOW?

As a nocturnal hunter, sound is just as important as sight for Tawny Owls. Its disc-like face directs sound waves to its ears which are hidden behind the feathers on either side of its head. These are slightly out of alignment with each other, which gives the owl its outstanding directional hearing and allows it to pinpoint prey so precisely in the dark.

SMALL OPEN-FRONTED NESTBOXES

OPEN-FRONTED NESTBOXES NEED TO BE PLACED IN WELL-CONCEALED LOCATIONS TO PREVENT EGGS AND CHICKS BEING EXPOSED TO THE THREAT OF PREDATORS AND BAD WEATHER.

ENTRANCE VARIATIONS

Overall dimensions for open-fronted boxes are identical to those with small hole entrances. The big difference concerns the front panel, which can be cut at one of three different heights, depending on which species you hope to attract.

● The medium height option (approx 100mm deep) will attract the widest range of birds, including the ever-popular Robin
● The high front (approx 140mm) is best for Wren
● The low front (approx 60mm) is best suited to Spotted Flycatchers.

ROOF

Access holes on the low and medium height fronts are large enough that nests can be inspected and cleaned without the need to remove the roof, so secure it firmly with nails or screws. In contrast, the high front option makes it far more diificult for you to reach down to completely remove all nest debris. For this style of box a removeable roof is the best solution, particularly if the nestbox has been positioned in a hard-to-reach spot.

If you opt to build the standard design with the roof higher at the back, make sure the overhang is large enough to deflect a lot of rain from entering the box.

Another design option, which is better at keeping the box interior dry, is to vary the heights of the side walls so that the roof slopes to one side. This may test your carpentry skills slightly more than the standard design, but it removes any danger of rain draining into the entrance.

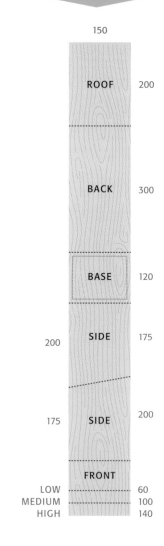

CUTTING TEMPLATE
Rough cut timber
Plank size: 150mm x 1095mm

150	
ROOF	200
BACK	300
BASE	120
SIDE	175
SIDE	200
FRONT	
LOW	60
MEDIUM	100
HIGH	140

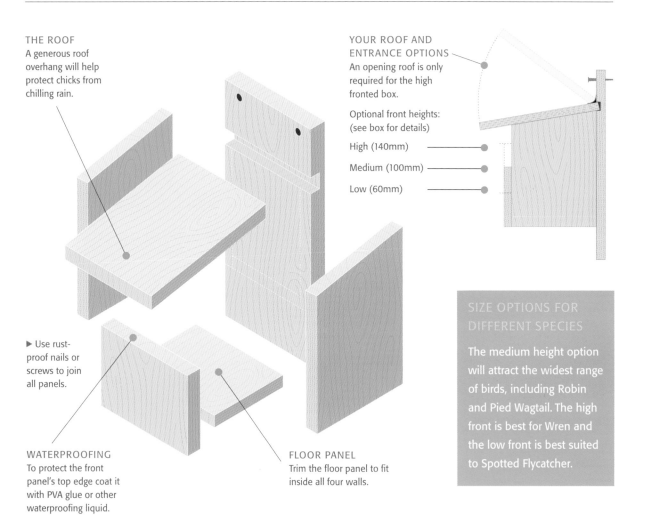

THE ROOF
A generous roof overhang will help protect chicks from chilling rain.

YOUR ROOF AND ENTRANCE OPTIONS
An opening roof is only required for the high fronted box.

Optional front heights:
(see box for details)

High (140mm)

Medium (100mm)

Low (60mm)

▶ Use rust-proof nails or screws to join all panels.

WATERPROOFING
To protect the front panel's top edge coat it with PVA glue or other waterproofing liquid.

FLOOR PANEL
Trim the floor panel to fit inside all four walls.

SIZE OPTIONS FOR DIFFERENT SPECIES

The medium height option will attract the widest range of birds, including Robin and Pied Wagtail. The high front is best for Wren and the low front is best suited to Spotted Flycatcher.

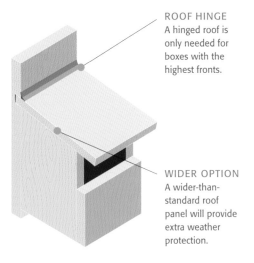

ROOF HINGE
A hinged roof is only needed for boxes with the highest fronts.

WIDER OPTION
A wider-than-standard roof panel will provide extra weather protection.

LOCATION

Eggs and chicks inside open-fronted boxes are at greater risk of being plundered by predators such as Magpies, Grey Squirrels and cats, so think carefully about the placement of your nestbox to minimise accessibility. Hiding a box inside or behind a shrub is one defence, or you could fix the box to a high wall that is out of reach of many predators.

If those options are not open to you, then consider fixing a stiff wire guard in front of the entrance. The gaps need to be large enough for the parent birds to enter freely, but small enough to exclude the hunters.

Robins are noted for picking nest sites that are well hidden, but Spotted Flycatchers prefer an open site to enable the sitting bird to have a good view of the surrounding area. Bear this in mind when siting your nestbox.

ROBIN
Erithacus rubecula

THE EVER-POPULAR ROBIN WAS A RUNAWAY WINNER OF A
NATIONAL POLL IN 2016 TO NOMINATE BRITAIN'S NATIONAL BIRD.

20mm

16mm

FACT FILE

HOW COMMON:
More than six million breeding
territories.

WHERE THEY LIVE:
Present in all parts of Britain and Ireland,
apart from some Scottish islands. Breeds
across a wide range of habitats.

NESTBOX TYPE:
Small open-fronted box – front panel
100mm in height.

NESTBOX LOCATION:
Hide nestbox with vegetation
at heights up to two metres.

HOW OFTEN THEY BREED:
Generally twice a year, but third broods
not unusual.

NEST MATERIALS:
A large cup of leaves, grass and
moss, lined with roots or animal hair.
Nests may be domed when built in
enclosed spaces.

EGGS:
4–5 white eggs with avariable
amount of speckling.

INCUBATION PERIOD:
14–15 – by female only.

NESTLINGS:
14–15 days before fledging.

There can be few lowland gardens in Britain that are not visited by Robins
on a daily basis and it was no surprise when the species was recently
adopted as our unofficial national bird after a public vote.

It is quite possible that you have already had Robins breeding in your
locality, but such is their skill at camouflage, pinpointing exactly where the
nest is located is no easy task. Their ingenuity is unbounded when it comes
to concealing their nest site: some will select holes or crevices which are
masked by Ivy, while others opt for holes in tree trunks, tree roots
or even beneath twigs under fallen leaf litter.

If your garden shed is of the ramshackle type, with permanent gaps in

CALENDAR	J	F	M	A	M	J	J	A	S	O	N	D
EGG LAYING:												
NESTLINGS:												

▲ Robins are bold defenders of their nesting territory: if singing does not deter a rival, they will fight.

the door or windows, you might well find a Robin has taken up residence, building a nest on a shelf or other suitable surface that is out of reach of predators. The abandoned nests of other species, such as Blackbird, may also be taken over by enterprising Robins.

HIDING FROM DANGER

To protect vulnerable chicks, you will need to be as conscientious as the parent Robins when deciding the location of an open-fronted box. Most Robins nest low down (under two metres from the ground), but your top priority is to find a place that is almost completely out of sight.

Boxes can be snuggled under over-hanging vegetation in a ditch or

Their ingenuity is unbounded when it comes to concealing their nest site: some will select holes or crevices which are masked by Ivy, while others opt for holes in tree trunks, tree roots or even beneath twigs in fallen leaf litter.

SPOT THE DIFFERENCE
Top left: Robin nests vary greatly
in size, depending on the
nestbox or cavity to be filled.
Above and left: Vulnerable young
Robins initially have a spotted
plumage to help camouflage
them from predators.

embankment, wedged deep into the fork of a thorny bush or behind a creeper
growing on a wall or fence. Don't worry about a clear flightpath to the nest
because Robins are quite happy to clamber through vegetation and watch
for predators before leaving the vicinity of the nest.

Robins are very adaptable and will vary the size of their nest to fit the
available space. If the first nesting attempt is successful, it is likely the Robins
will choose the same nestbox for their following broods.

AN ALTERNATIVE DESIGN

An alternative design which is also very suitable for Robins is a small box with
a 65mm diameter entrance hole: this may offer the chicks a slightly better
level of protection from both weather and predators. One thing you should
avoid doing is providing nestboxes made of metal or ceramic: Robins are often
depicted nesting in 'cute' objects such as kettles or teapots, but these are far
more prone to condensation and offer less insulation than wooden boxes.

DID YOU KNOW?

Robins may appear to be
fearless when they hop around
your feet looking for food, but
they exhibit extreme degrees
of caution when it comes to
the breeding season.

For example, if a female
suspects you are watching
her while she's carrying nest
material, she is likely to make
visits to different parts of the
garden to disguise the location
of the true nest site.

PIED WAGTAIL
Motacilla alba

A SPECIES THAT OFTEN LIVES CLOSE TO WATER, THE PIED WAGTAIL
OCCUPIES HABITATS WITH OPEN GROUND AND SHORT VEGETATION.

21mm

15mm

While some species seem to have very precise needs when it comes
to nest sites, Pied Wagtails are supremely adaptable. They will happily take
to nestboxes of varying sizes and shapes and left to their own devices they
will build nests in piles of wood or stone, in unused drainpipes, holes in
walls, on machinery in farm buildings and under bridges.

MULTIPLE NESTBOX CHOICES

This adaptability means you do not need to slavishly follow any particular
design for your nestbox as long as you ensure that the nesting cavity inside

FACT FILE

HOW COMMON:
More than 460,000 breeding pairs.

WHERE THEY LIVE:
A resident subspecies of White Wagtail,
found in all parts of Britain and Ireland.
Favours open habitats.

NESTBOX TYPE:
Small open-fronted box – front panel
100mm in height.

NESTBOX LOCATION:
Nestboxes may be placed up to 5m
above ground level on buildings
or trees, preferably close to areas
of grass and water.

HOW OFTEN THEY BREED:
Usually twice a year, but on rare
occasions a third brood is attempted.

NEST MATERIALS:
Twigs, roots and moss, lined with locally
available materials.

EGGS:
5–6 greyish eggs with brown speckles.

INCUBATION PERIOD:
12–14 days – by both parent birds.

NESTLINGS:
13–16 days before fledging.

CALENDAR	J	F	M	A	M	J	J	A	S	O	N	D
EGG LAYING:												
NESTLINGS:												

▲ A juvenile Pied Wagtail, which is predominantly brown, begs for food from its parent.

is at least as large as the standard nestbox dimensions. The entrance hole should be a 50mm x 50mm square. To save making a nestbox from new wood, it is perfectly okay to adapt a wooden packing crate… just ensure it is waterproof.

WIDE-RANGING HABITAT CHOICES

In the wild, Pied Wagtails will nest at various heights but most successful nestboxes will be between one and five metres above the ground. Pied Wagtails are comfortable around humans and you may have seen them foraging for food in car parks and other urban areas.

Pied Wagtails are versatile enough to be successful in a wide range of habitats that can offer areas of open ground and short vegetation where insect prey can be seen easily. Some nest on moorland edge and mixed farmland but they will readily use nestboxes attached to buildings, particularly if they are close to ponds, streams or other water sources.

Other natural nests have been discovered in quarries, rocky islets and sea cliffs, while in gardens some wagtails have chosen to build nests in plant pots and abandoned Blackbird nests.

DID YOU KNOW?

A subspecies of Europe's White Wagtail, the Pied Wagtail is resident in southern Britain, but birds that have bred in northern Scotland and uplands in England and Wales will migrate to lower ground in winter.

In some towns, winter flocks of several thousand birds will roost together in trees.

WREN
Troglodytes troglodytes

WRENS MAY USE YOUR NESTBOX AS A WARM WINTER ROOST
AS WELL AS FOR ITS SUMMERTIME BREEDING POSSIBILITIES.

17mm

13mm

FACT FILE

HOW COMMON:
Around 7.7 million breeding territories
makes the Wren the most common bird
species in Britain.

WHERE THEY LIVE:
Found in all parts of Britain and Ireland
and across a wide range of habitats.

NESTBOX TYPE:
Small open-fronted box –
front panel 140mm in height.

NESTBOX LOCATION:
Well hidden, preferably in thick,
thorny undergrowth.

HOW OFTEN THEY BREED:
Twice a year, but only once
in northern Britain.

NEST MATERIALS:
A domed structure of leaves, moss
and grass, lined with feathers.

EGGS:
5–6 white eggs, some with fine
speckles or reddish-brown spots.

INCUBATION PERIOD:
13–18 days – by female only.

NESTLINGS:
14–19 days before fledging.

Discretion lies at the heart of the Wren's breeding success. Its tiny size
means it is well-equipped for moving through dense vegetation and it will often
build its own nest in the heart of a prickly bush or bramble that is out of reach
of other species. If you have Berberis or Pyracantha bushes in your garden,
wedge a nestbox into the densest part of the plant.

STANDARD SIZE IS BEST

Stick with the standard measurements given for our small open-fronted
nestboxes. Wrens always construct nest chambers of the same size at the

CALENDAR	J	F	M	A	M	J	J	A	S	O	N	D
EGG LAYING:												
NESTLINGS:												

Male Wrens have a
surprisingly loud song,
considering their small
body size, and will use
it along with aggressive
postures to deter other
males from entering
their chosen territory.

NEST CHOICES
Above: Wrens will sometimes build nests inside boxes with small hole entrances if they are well hidden from potential predators.
Left: Feeding hungry chicks at a well-hidden natural nest site.

heart of the box, so if you provide larger boxes the parent birds will have to spend time gathering materials to fill the extra space.

Male Wrens have a busy start to the breeding season, building several unlined 'cock nests'. Eventually the female will choose one and line it with feathers. If you find a 'cock nest' in your nestbox, try putting three or four more boxes within a few metres because the male Wren is quite likely to select one of these for a later nest.

WINTER REFUGES FROM THE COLD

In most cases just a few Wrens will snuggle together, but there was an amazing record of 61 birds crammed into a single Norfolk nestbox in 1969. You may never be aware of this happening in your garden as birds enter the boxes after sunset and leave before dawn.

Wrens will sometimes adopt a nestbox with a small entrance hole (generally 28mm diameter or above) if you place it in a well hidden site where it won't be discovered by tits or sparrows. When building nests in hedgerows, Wrens will carefully choose dead leaves, moss and grass to blend in with the surroundings. In nestboxes and other small cavities the domed roof will not be completed.

DID YOU KNOW?

Because Wrens rarely wander from their home areas, birds in far-flung places tend to develop different characteristics and eventually become distinct subspecies. Four of the six subspecies of UK Wren which have developed since the last Ice Age are island races, found on Shetland, Fair Isle, St Kilda and the Outer Hebrides. A fifth is found across the northern and western mainland, intergrading with a sixth in the south-east of England.

SPOTTED FLYCATCHER
Muscicapa striata

SPOTTED FLYCATCHERS ARRIVE LATE FROM AFRICA BUT SOME PAIRS
MANAGE TO RAISE TWO FAMILIES BEFORE DEPARTING IN SEPTEMBER.

19mm

14mm

A steady decline in Spotted Flycatcher numbers since the 1960s
accelerated to the point that the UK population plummeted by 89% between
1967 and 2010. Not surprisingly, Spotted Flycatcher has now been red-listed
as a bird of conservation concern.

Quite why Spotted Flycatcher populations have declined so dramatically
is unclear. The survival of chicks during their first year of life has decreased,
and may have contributed to the decline seen. Interestingly, breeding success
in gardens appears to be better than that observed in woodland or farmland
habitats. Nest predation and a decline in the availability of favoured insect
prey may also be important, as could conditions on the wintering grounds.

Spotted Flycatchers will breed in many different habitats where there
are large deciduous trees, but they prefer a nest site with a clear outlook,
so position your box to look over a lawn, or woodland glade. Ideally,

FACT FILE

HOW COMMON:
Serious decline to around 33,000
breeding territories.

WHERE THEY LIVE:
Found in most parts of Britain and
Ireland apart from some Scottish islands.
Favours woodland, woodland edge and
rural gardens.

NESTBOX TYPE:
Small open-fronted box – front panel
60mm in height.

NESTBOX LOCATION:
Erect at heights between two and four
metres above ground in places with
clear views.

HOW OFTEN THEY BREED:
Once a year, but second broods
possible.

NEST MATERIALS:
Twigs, roots and moss, lined with locally
available materials.

EGGS:
4–5 off-white eggs, usually with
reddish mottling.

INCUBATION PERIOD:
12–14 days – mostly by female.

NESTLINGS:
Usually around 13 days before fledging.

CALENDAR	J	F	M	A	M	J	J	A	S	O	N	D
EGG LAYING:												
NESTLINGS:												

▲ A sturdy open-fronted box partly hidden by shrubbery, for protection against predators, makes a very safe nest option.

position the box under a branch, so that hanging leaves mask its position but still allow the sitting bird to have good views. Boxes secreted into creepers on a house wall also make successful locations.

PROVIDE PLENTY OF PERCHES

This species hunts by watching flying insects from a favoured perch, then catching them in the air. If successful, it will return to the perch before taking the food to the nest. It is therefore necessary to ensure there are several clear perches close to your nestbox.

Spotted Flycatchers are adaptable when choosing nest locations and if nestboxes are not available, they may build one inside a large hole in an old wall, or even in a hanging basket, if there is enough foliage to hide its position.

If there is not enough plant cover available, you can provide some protection from predators by fitting a screen of 50mm chicken wire over the front of the box. The parent birds are small enough to slip through the wire, but it should deter larger birds and some animals. Do not add wire when nesting has started.

This species hunts by watching flying insects from a favoured perch, then catching them in the air. If successful, it will return to the perch before taking the food to the nest.

SWIFT
Apus apus

HOUSE RENOVATIONS HAVE BEEN BAD NEWS FOR BREEDING
SWIFTS, BUT NESTBOXES CAN HELP REDRESS THE BALANCE.

25mm

16mm

We do not know why Swift numbers have declined by 51% since 1995
but modern building design, coupled with the refurbishment of old buildings,
may deprive Swifts of nest sites and be contributing to population decline.

Various organisations work to raise awareness of the birds' plight and
proactive groups, such as Action for Swifts, Swift Conservation and members
of the Swifts Local Network encourage the provision of more nest boxes by
offering information via their websites.

Enthusiastic volunteers work with land and property owners to install large
scale nestbox schemes. For instance, Swift Conservation has installed boxes
at London railway stations and on a restored church in Reading, Berkshire.

FACT FILE

HOW COMMON:
From an estimated 87,000 breeding
pairs in 2009, Swifts have declined
by 4% per annum.

WHERE THEY LIVE:
Widespread in towns and villages,
absent or scarce in NW Scotland.

WHERE THEY NEST:
Usually in buildings, rarely in tree
or cliff cavities in the UK.

NESTBOX TYPE:
A cavity box with oblong, obround
or half-moon entrance near the floor.

NESTBOX LOCATION:
External under eaves, internal in Swift
bricks, or inside roof spaces in gable ends.
Preferably five metres above ground level.

HOW OFTEN THEY BREED:
Once a year.

NEST MATERIALS:
A low-sided cup made of anything floating
in the air, mainly feathers and vegetable
matter, cemented with saliva.

EGGS:
2–3 white eggs.

INCUBATION PERIOD:
19–26 days – by both sexes.

NESTLINGS:
37–56 days before fledging,
depending on the weather.

CALENDAR	J	F	M	A	M	J	J	A	S	O	N	D
EGG LAYING:												
NESTLINGS:												

▲ An adult Swift returns to a nestbox with its crop bulging with insects to be fed to its hungry chick.

SIZE IS NOT IMPORTANT

You can site your boxes under the eaves or inside your loft with just the entrance hole showing externally. If you have any plans to renew a roof, it may be possible to incorporate boxes on top of the wall, accessed under the eaves.

Internal nestboxes are preferred by Swifts: they are more secure and more thermally stable. The exact shape and size of the box is not important as Swifts can nest in very confined spaces, but aim for a minimum floor area of 350cm², minimum width of 12cm and a minimum headroom of 7.5cm.

Swifts are happy to nest in close proximity to each other and in some places, particularly in Europe, enthusiasts have built multi-chambered nest terraces to fit into the gable ends of their homes.

> The exact shape and size of the box is not important as Swifts can nest in very confined spaces, but you will probably have more success if you can make the nesting area at the back of the box wider and slightly higher than the entrance end.

INTERIOR SWIFT BOX

A STRAIGHTFORWARD DESIGN
FOR FITTING INTO ATTICS
OR ROOF SPACES.

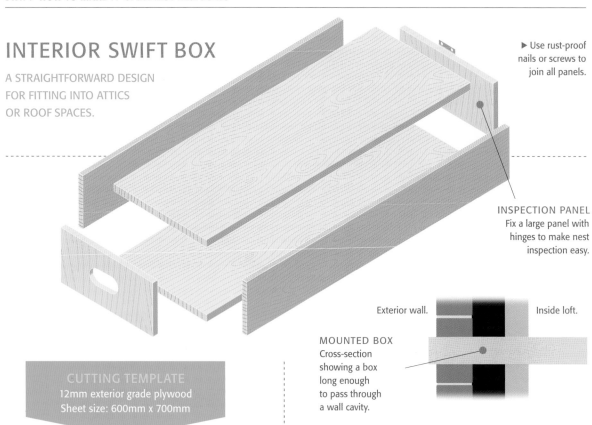

▶ Use rust-proof
nails or screws to
join all panels.

INSPECTION PANEL
Fix a large panel with
hinges to make nest
inspection easy.

Exterior wall.   Inside loft.

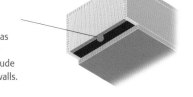

MOUNTED BOX
Cross-section
showing a box
long enough
to pass through
a wall cavity.

CUTTING TEMPLATE
12mm exterior grade plywood
Sheet size: 600mm x 700mm

600

BASE	200
TOP	200
SIDE	100
SIDE	100
BACK ◀ FRONT	100

175   175

**ENTRANCE
OPTIONS**
This gap in the
floor panel acts as
the entrance for
boxes that protrude
through cavity walls.

STANDARD AND ENLARGED BOX DESIGNS

The dimensions of our standard nestbox can be increased. Adding
a large nest chamber will make inspection and cleaning much easier.

INSIDE THE BOX
Above: If space allows, it pays to build
a bigger nest chamber to give easier
access for cleaning.
Right: A fast-growing chick rests in a
concave while a parent keeps watch
through the entrance hole.

You can increase occupancy rates and the chances of Swifts breeding in
the first year they discover the nestbox if you install a shallow dish-shaped
nesting cup called a 'concave'. There are several ways to construct a concave:

- Cut a 8.5cm hole in the centre of a 12cm square piece of MDF or plywood
  and glue it to the floor of your box. Use sandpaper to soften the edge of
  the cut circle.
- A softer material, such as fibre-board is easier to work with when making
  a concave scoop with a vertical rim. Coat the finished concave with PVA
  glue to deter sparrows and tits pecking pieces out of it.
- Build the 8.5cm diameter concave shape from papier mache.
  When the concave is placed inside your box, scatter small, soft feathers
  for the Swifts to complete their nest.

If you opt for an outside box make sure it is weatherproof. Boxes made
of wood or plywood are best installed under broad eaves, away from sun
and rain, but if you can only use a more exposed position give the box a
sloping roof made of a waterproof material. If exposed to the sun, the roof
needs to be at least 20mm thick and painted white. Nestboxes can face
any direction, including south, with entrances placed horizontally, obliquely
downward or vertically downward.

The entrance should be an oblong or obround (a slot with rounded ends)

▲ Swift chicks are able to enter a form
of torpor during periods of poor weather,
when there is less food available.

measuring 65mm x 28mm. Anything larger may allow Starlings to take over the nest. There is no way of preventing House Sparrows or tits from using a Swift nestbox, but you may be able to diffuse potential conflicts by putting up more conventional boxes for these other species.

Ideally, boxes should be placed five metres above ground level, because lower elevations may decrease the chances of occupancy. Obstructions in front of the box, particularly trees, should be avoided.

CLEAN WITH CAUTION

In normal circumstances, Swifts spend the first year that they occupy a nestbox building a nest in preparation for the following year. It is therefore important not to clean out old nests. Sometimes another species such as House Sparrow might bring in nesting material, but Swifts can nest on top of this.

Invertebrates will reduce the amount of nest material over the winter. A heavy infestation of Crataerina pupae may be removed, but these blood-sucking parasites are not known to cause any measurable harm to Swifts.

Swifts are among the last migrant species to arrive each spring. Breeding birds nearly always return to the same nest; interestingly young Swifts do not

Ideally, boxes should be placed five metres above ground level, because lower elevations may decrease the chances of occupancy. Obstructions in front of the box, particularly trees, should be avoided.

INTERIOR OR EXTERIOR BOXES - IT'S YOUR CHOICE

EXTERIOR ALTERNATIVES

A number of exterior box designs featured on the two websites mentioned on page 115 can be adapted to suit your own house. This simple rectangular box is best made from 12mm thick exterior quality plywood. Place a concave on the floor furthest away from the entrance hole to avoid the risk of eggs rolling out.

The outside of the box can be painted to blend in with your brickwork, but leave the inside natural. If you have House Sparrows in your locality you may be able to deter them from taking up residence by locating the entrance hole on the underside of your box.

breed until they are three or even four years of age. If their old nesting sites have been destroyed, replacement boxes will often attract new tenants.

A sure-fire way to get the attention of Swifts searching for new nest sites is to play recordings of their calls through a tweeter located near or in your boxes. Visit the Action For Swifts website for full details on how to install and use these devices for maximum effect.

Young Swifts occupy their first nest sites during June and July, so boxes need to be in place by the end of May. If you are providing replacement boxes for mature breeding birds then the first week of May is your deadline. Inspection at the end of the season should be carried out cautiously because some Swifts do not depart until well into August or even September.

At the same website you will find instructions on how to build a variety of Swift nest boxes suitable for indoors or the exterior of buildings.

ON-LINE EXPERT ADVICE

Thanks to the efforts of dedicated conservation volunteers, knowledge about the specific needs of Swifts is growing all the time. For more information visit actionforswifts.blogspot.com or swift-conservation.org.

DID YOU KNOW?

Swifts spend almost all their life on the wing, eating, sleeping and mating. They only come to 'land' to nest. Their legs are short, with strong feet and sharp claws, giving them a grip when they land and enabling them to crawl inside their nestboxes.

British Swifts, which migrate to Africa each year, may fly 300,000 miles non-stop between fledging late one summer and landing at a potential nest site two summers later.

BUILT-IN OPTIONS

If you are having a new house or an extension built then consider incorporating special entrance bricks in the exterior wall to allow access to Swift nestboxes in the loft space. This illustration shows a cavity wall building where a plastic soil pipe acts as the linking tunnel between entrance hole and a tall rectangular nest chamber.

Before any building work gets underway it is worth contacting either of the Swift conservation groups mentioned above. These enthusiasts, who have done so much to promote the welfare of Swifts will be happy to work with you to install the best design for your situation.

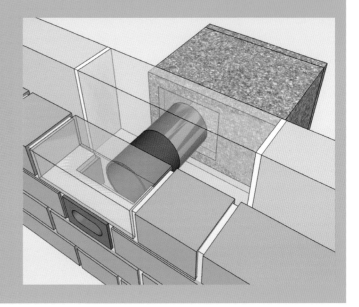

BARN OWL
Tyto alba

ERECTING NESTBOXES IN SUITABLE HUNTING HABITAT IS ESSENTIAL
IF BRITAIN'S FRAGILE POPULATION OF BARN OWLS IS TO RECOVER.

40mm

32mm

Variety is the name of the game when it comes to catering for the nesting needs of one of Britain's most beautiful birds. A lack of suitable nest sites in certain parts of the country has contributed to a drop in nesting opportunities, so any nestboxes you can provide, if there is suitable hunting habitat around, will be a great contribution to conservation.

BOX CHARACTERISTICS

The cutting diagram gives a rectangular design which can be made from FSC-approved exterior grade 12mm plywood. If you have an indoor location for your box you can get away with 9mm thickness wood. Treat the cutting plan measurements as the absolute minimum, because Barn Owls will happily take over spaces much larger than this. The real limitation is your ability to manouvre the box onto position.

Ready-made boxes, such as sturdy tea chests, can be used as alternatives to building your own from plywood, but they will need to be adapted to fit in with our recommended design. Position the entrance hole above halfway up on the box front to discourage young chicks from making a premature exit before they can fly.

As the chicks grow to full size, space inside the box will become limited. It will help the birds if you add an external platform below the entrance hole where the entire brood can exercise and await food deliveries, while minimising the danger of them falling to the ground before fledging.

As adult Barn Owls will not collect any nesting material of their own, it will help them adopt a new box if you line it with a 3mm deep layer of wood shavings. Pellets regurgitated by the adults will eventually contribute to the nest lining.

FACT FILE

HOW COMMON:
Estimated at around 4,000 breeding pairs in the UK, down from 12,000 in 1932, but no longer amber-listed as a species of conservation concern. Breeding success can fall or rise dramatically depending on availability of prey.

WHERE THEY LIVE
Widespread in Britain and Ireland, but generally absent from uplands and urban areas.

NESTBOX TYPE:
Large box with special entrance hole and internal compartment to offer chicks more security.

NESTBOX LOCATION:
Fix to isolated trees or poles at heights above four metres with clear flight paths to the entrance. Boxes can also be fixed to beams or the walls of barns and other agricultural buildings.

HOW OFTEN THEY BREED:
Once or twice a year, depending on the availability of prey.

NEST MATERIALS:
Barn Owls add no soft material to nestboxes, but may make a hollow in natural tree cavities.

EGGS:
4–6 white eggs.

INCUBATION PERIOD:
32 days – by female only.

NESTLINGS:
53–61 days before fledging.

CALENDAR	J	F	M	A	M	J	J	A	S	O	N	D
EGG LAYING:												
NESTLINGS:												

▲ To save energy in winter, Barn Owls will often drop down on mice or voles from perches rather than constantly scour grassland from the air.

BOXES IN BUILDINGS

A box located inside a building offers the best protection from adverse weather and the risk of disturbance. It is also probable that positioning and fixing a box inside a solid structure will be a lot easier and more convenient compared to lugging ladders, ropes and the box to a quiet spot in the country.

If you can get access to a barn or other rural building, site the box so that its entrance hole is facing towards the window or door mostly likely to be used by the incoming owl. The box should not be positioned lower than three metres above ground level to minimise disturbance.

A lack of suitable nest sites in certain parts of the country has contributed to a drop in Barn Owl nesting opportunities.

BARN OWL BOX

NESTBOXES DESTINED TO BE PLACED
INSIDE OLD FARM BUILDINGS CAN
BE LESS WATERPROOF AND STURDY
THAN OUTDOOR BOXES

FLUSH ROOF
The roof of an indoor
box does not need
to overhang the
entrance hole.

ENTRANCE POSITION
Place the 150mm square entrance hole
high to stop chicks leaving prematurely.

CUTTING TEMPLATE
12mm exterior grade plywood
Sheet size: 945mm x 2120mm

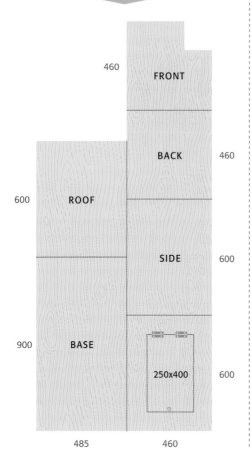

**LANDING
PLATFORM**
Glue wooden battens
to the edge to make the
platform more stable.

INSPECTION PANEL
Choose the location
for an inspection panel
based on where the box
will be placed indoors.

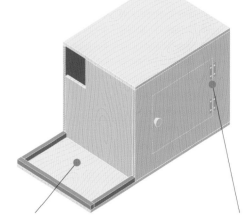

PLATFORM PERCH
Young Barn Owls will
appreciate a place where
they can stretch out.

HINGE OPTIONS
Hinges on the side of
an inspection panel.

▶ Fix nails or screws into wooden battens previously glued into position.

GROWING FAMILIES
It is not unusual for Barn Owls to lay up to
six eggs, and if a majority survive then the
interior of a nestbox is likely to seem very
crowded. Making your box larger than our
standard size design will give them more
space, while a platform below the entrance
hole will be used as an exercise zone once
the chicks grow flight feathers.

For boxes placed onto a cross beam, deter cats from approaching by tying
holly or other thorny twigs along its length. Avoid positioning the box directly
over any stored foodstuff to prevent contamination from their droppings.

Carrying large boxes up ladders and then fixing them in place is not the
easiest of tasks, so with safety at the front of your mind, it is best to seek out
local experts to supervise erection of your box. For more detailed advice on
how to fix boxes safely within buildings, visit the website of the Barn Owl Trust
(www.barnowltrust.org.uk).

If you know of an upcoming barn conversion in a nearby rural area,
encourage the owner to consider installing a Barn Owl box in the loft space,
but only if there is suitable hunting habitat close by. Owls need constant
access to the box, so a permanent hole in the wall is better than a door or
window which might be occasionally shut.

Barn Owls like to have separate nesting and roosting sites, so two boxes
in a territory will be helpful.

> Carrying large boxes up
> ladders and then fixing
> them in place is not the
> easiest of tasks, so it is
> best to seek out local
> experts to supervise
> erection of your box.

A-SHAPE IS BEST SHAPE
A number of companies now offer ready-built A-frame boxes for Barn Owls and they have proved very successful in a variety of outdoor locations. Left: maturing chicks wander out onto a landing platform to exercise their wings.

BOXES IN TREES

Barn Owls frequently make nests in large tree holes, so will certainly occupy a nestbox if it fulfils certain conditions:

- The tree, either an isolated one in a hedgerow or on the edge of a wood, needs to be in a quiet spot where the birds are not likely to be disturbed.
- The tree's trunk should be substantial enough to cope with the weight of the box.
- Choose trees with a high canopy and no low-down branches.
- In undisturbed locations boxes can be as low as 3.5 metres above ground.
- Glue roofing felt to the roof for extra protection.
- Avoid placing a box within a kilometre of a major road because Barn Owls that hunt along roadside verges often end up as traffic casualities.

There is no point in erecting nestboxes for Barn Owls if there is little or no suitable hunting territory close at hand. The ideal habitat is mixed farmland, with plenty of rough grass field margins or drainage ditches where rodents will be plentiful.

TOP TIP
As Barn Owls will often choose large tree holes for nest holes, check your local area for tall broken stumps where a nestbox might be placed.

ALTERNATIVE OUTDOOR OPTION

Triangular-shaped nestboxes have become increasingly popular in recent years for outdoor locations, either mounted on poles or fixed to trees or buildings. Making your own version may challenge your woodworking skills because the battens used to reinforce the joints need to be bevelled. The front panel also needs to be removeable, so that you can more easily screw the box to its support.

A simpler option is to buy a ready-made box from one of several manufacturers which advertise on the internet. Even then, seek help from a local licensed Barn Owl expert when it comes to fixing a box in place and hopefully to monitor the growth of a new family of owls.

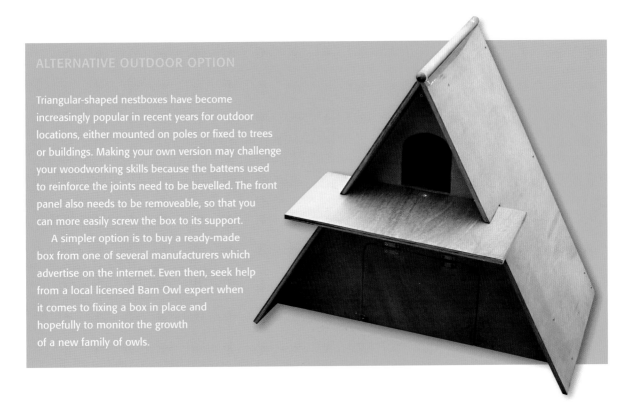

Even exterior-grade plywood will swell and split if not thoroughly protected from rain, so it is important to use a waterproof sealant when fixing battens to all the box joints. To protect the edges of all plywood panels, coat with sealant or glue and let them dry before assembly.

Use rust-proof screws to build the box and set the floor panel above the bottom of the side panels to stop water collecting. Just to be on the safe side, drill some 20mm holes in the floor in case rain does enter through the entrance hole.

CLEANING AND INSPECTION

Barn Owl is a Schedule 1 species, which means you need a licence to inspect an occupied nestbox. A hinged door on a side panel usually gives the best access for cleaning, but this is not necessary every year if occupied solely by Barn Owls. However, boxes are often taken over by Stock Doves, Kestrels or Jackdaws and the latter species in particular will bring in a lot of nesting material, including twigs, so ensure the box is emptied fully at the end of their breeding cycle.

Once cleaning is completed, sprinkle a few of the removed pellets on the nestbox floor to encourage re-occupancy.

Even exterior-grade plywood will swell and split if not thoroughly protected from rain, so it is important to use a waterproof sealant when fixing battens to all the box joints.

KESTREL
Falco tinnunculus

KESTRELS CHOOSE VARIED NATURAL NEST SITES – CLIFF LEDGES, BROKEN TREE SNAGS AND ABANDONED CROW'S NESTS ARE ALL SUITABLE.

40mm

32mm

The Kestrel has lost its position as Britain's most widespread bird of prey to the rapidly-expanding Common Buzzard, but the reasons for its decline are not fully understood.

Within recent memory it was almost impossible to make a car journey along an A-road without seeing one of these attractive falcons hovering over the roadside verges, intently looking for shrews and voles. Unfortunately, the increasing use of rodenticides and changes in agricultural practices may have contributed to the Kestrel's decline by reducing prey numbers.

A lack of suitable natural nest sites may also be a factor, so if you have the opportunity to fix a box near open fields, you may be plugging a gap in that particular locality. Kestrels are not restricted to using cavities and so may also use old Crow nests, but these can suffer from exposure to wind and rain, so a well-positioned nestbox is always a good option.

THE HIGHER THE BETTER

When looking for potential sites, remember that Kestrels like to have good views from the nestbox as well as a clear flightpath to it. Position the box as high as you can safely manage to improve the birds' vantage point and to keep it clear of human interference. Some birds have occupied boxes as low at 2.5 metres from the ground, but five metres high is the ideal.

A nestbox of the recommended size needs to be strong enough to withstand the battering of wind and heavy rain, so don't compromise on the quality of the materials you use. Finish the job by adding a stout pole or branch across the front of the box, extending to the side far enough to allow adult and juvenile birds to perch and keep a look-out.

Though primarily a design that will suit Kestrels, other species such

FACT FILE

HOW COMMON:
The most widespread bird of prey in Ireland, but the British population has declined to around 45,000 breeding pairs, leading to it being amber-listed as a bird of conservation concern.

WHERE THEY LIVE:
Widely found in open grassland and farmland across the UK, but scarce in NW Scotland and parts of central Wales.

NESTBOX TYPE:
Large open-fronted box with perching pole, situated to give clear views.

NESTBOX LOCATION:
Fix to trees at heights above five metres with clear flight paths to the entrance. Increasing in urban areas and may occupy boxes fixed to buildings.

HOW OFTEN THEY BREED:
Once a year.

NEST MATERIALS:
Kestrels bring little or no soft material to the nest site, but the box is likely to fill with prey remains and pellets.

EGGS:
4–5 white eggs, but often so heavily marked with reddish-brown speckles that the white is obscured.

INCUBATION PERIOD:
27–29 days – by female only.

NESTLINGS:
27–32 days before fledging.

CALENDAR	J	F	M	A	M	J	J	A	S	O	N	D
EGG LAYING:												
NESTLINGS:												

▲ Although a bird of open country, Kestrels may use waste ground in urban areas.

KESTREL BOX

WEATHERPROOFING IS THE KEY TO GIVING LARGE NESTBOXES A LONG AND USEFUL LIFE.

DRAINAGE HOLES
Drill holes in the floor to let excess moisture drain away.

STURDY PERCH
A long, strong perch will be used by both adult and immature Kestrels.

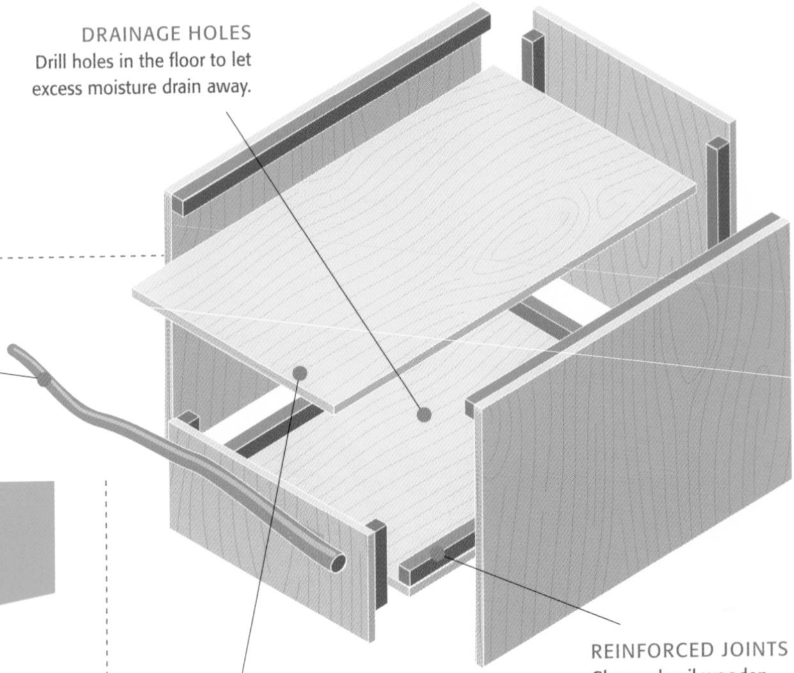

CUTTING TEMPLATE
12mm exterior grade plywood
Sheet size: 600mm x 1200mm

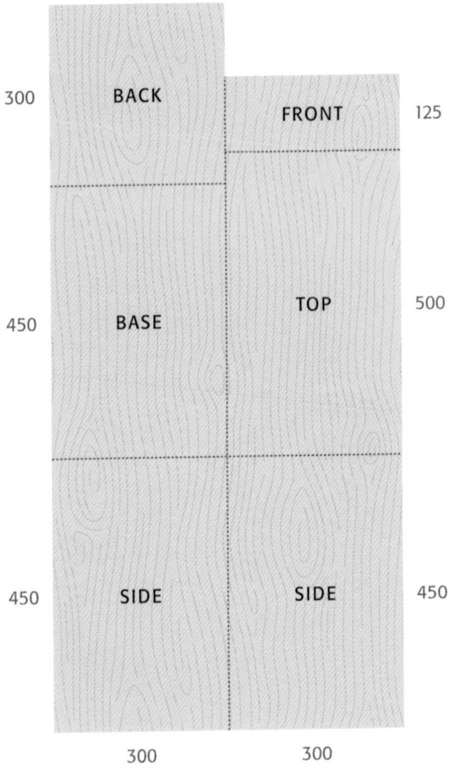

ROOF OVERHANG
Provide a generous overhang for extra protection from sun and rain.

REINFORCED JOINTS
Glue and nail wooden battens at joints to increase box life.

300	BACK
	FRONT 125
450	BASE
	TOP 500
450	SIDE
	SIDE 450
300	300

WATERPROOFING
Waterproof the edge of this panel with PVA glue.

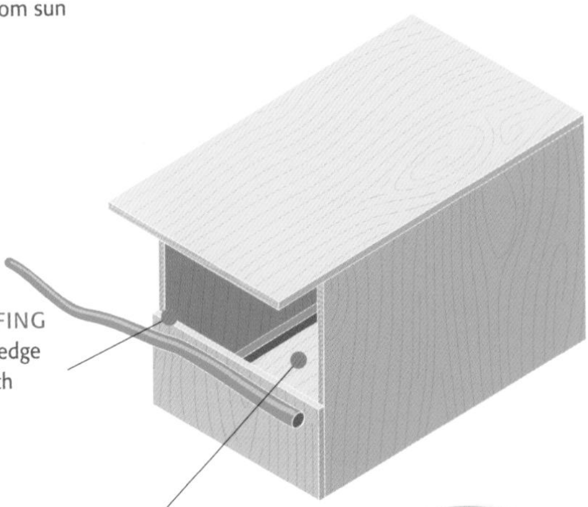

NESTBOX ANGLE
Ideally, the floor of the box will tilt down at the back.

TOP TIP
Construct these boxes well and you will find that they will last for a good many years.

▶ Fix rust-proof screws into wooden battens previously glued into position.

▲ A young family of Kestrels, though not yet ready to fly, take advantage of a perch to exercise away from the confines of their nestbox.

as Stock Doves, Jackdaws and Tawny Owls have all beeen recorded nesting in this type of box.

Studies in Finland have shown that Kestrels are more likely to occupy nestboxes located close to grassy ditches (a favoured hunting habitat) than those near forests, houses or roads. A similar approach is likely to be beneficial here in the UK, with boxes positioned in farmland or other open country close to suitable hunting habitat.

Some pairs have even been known to nest on deeply recessed window ledges, but if you see that happening it is a good idea to fix a barrier across the front of the window sill to prevent eggs accidentally rolling over the edge.

CONSTRUCTION

The best material for building a box of this type is 12mm exterior grade plywood, as it strikes the right balance between weight and sturdiness. Constructing a large box from sawn timber planks will result in something so heavy it will pose a serious danger to you when trying to fix it high in a tree.

Kestrels do not build nests for themselves. They will use old Carrion Crow nests, but as these can suffer from exposure to wind and rain, a well-positioned nestbox is always a better option.

HEIGHT AND DIRECTION THE KEYS TO SUCCESS

▲ Kestrel nestboxes need to be fixed securely to posts to withstand extreme winds. Below: Fit an extra wooden panel to secure boxes to trees.

Kestrels will choose natural nest sites on a cliff edge, building ledge, in disused stick nests or tree hollows, so can be attracted to nestboxes in different situations where prey is likely to be found. Local land-owners and farmers will probably welcome you fixing a Kestrel box on their estate as the birds will help keep rodent numbers in check.

Nestboxes can be fixed to isolated trees, woodland edges or buildings, but whatever the location it needs to be placed high so that the adult falcons can keep a close eye on their surroundings. Avoid siting the box above water-filled ditches, which may present a hazard to chicks if they were to fall from the box. Traffic is less of a problem for Kestrels than for Barn Owls, so it is acceptable to place boxes near to roads.

INSIDE THE NESTBOX
Above: A nestbox designed by the Hawk & Owl
Trust. Right: High numbers of field voles will be
needed to enable parent Kestrels to feed five
youngsters until they fledge.

There are ready-made boxes available commercially which use weather-resistent plywood. Fixing nails into the end section of plywood will lead to splitting, seriously shortening the useful life of these large boxes, so fix 20mm wood battens at each joint to accommodate the screws in a secure manner.

MOUNTING THE BOX

Boxes with large openings are vulnerable in high winds, so screw your box to a strong wooden board that can be fixed securely to a tree.

Kestrels will generally make their nest in the darkest part of the box, away from the entrance to the box. If you position the box so that the floor tilts slightly backwards, this will stop eggs rolling forward in the nest.

DRAINAGE AND WATERPROOFING

Ensure the opening to the nestbox doesn't point in the direction of the most prevalent rain and wind. Even with a generous overlap on the roof, most boxes of this type will admit some rainwater and it will pay to drill a series of drainage holes in the floor to remove excess wetness.

Protect the outside of the box with a coating of waterproof preservative and use roofing felt (the type more normally used for garden sheds), to cover the roof of the box. Use waterproof glue on all the joints to minimise water damage.

Boxes with large openings are vulnerable in high winds, so screw your box to a strong wooden board that can be fixed securely to a tree.

PAPIER-MÂCHÉ NESTBOXES

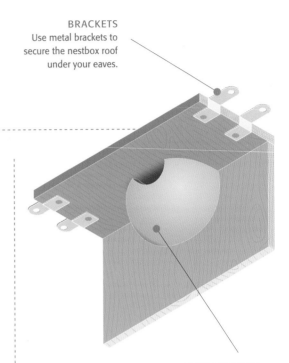

BRACKETS
Use metal brackets to secure the nestbox roof under your eaves.

NEST POSITION
Nest cups for House Martins need to fit flush with the roof panel.

MAKING NEST CUPS FROM PAPIER-MÂCHÉ IS A FUN THING TO DO WITH CHILDREN. THE SHAPE OF THE FINISHED CUP IS NOT CRITICAL, BUT VARNISH IT TO ENSURE IT IS WATERPROOF AND LONG-LASTING.

PAPER PULP METHOD

To make your nest cup from paper pulp, you will need the following:
- Wooden backboard.
- Wooden roof panel (if your target species is House Martin).
- Clay or Plasticine for making a mould.
- Torn-up egg cartons or newspaper soaked in wallpaper paste.
- Vaseline for greasing the inside of the mould.
- Thin metal tabs or bent metal strip for fixing the cup to a wooden backboard.

STEP-BY-STEP INSTRUCTIONS

- Soak torn-up newspaper or toilet paper overnight in wallpaper paste. Follow instructions for mixing the paste, but add slightly less water than recommended
- Make a cup-shaped mould from clay (or Plasticine) slightly larger than you want the finished nest cup to be.
- Grease mould with Vaseline so the finished papier mâché cup can be removed easily when dry.
- Squeeze out excess water from the paper pulp and then press it into the mould. Aim for a thickness of at least one centimetre.
- Insert metal tabs into the papier mâché (see diagram) to help fix the cup to a backboard.
- Once dry, remove the cup from the mould and varnish with PVA glue (or similar waterproof coating) inside and out.
- Trim any rough edges to ensure the cup fits tightly to the backboard and roof panels.

ADDING METAL MOUNTING STRIPS TO YOUR CUP MOULDS

Embed a strip of thin metal between layers of papier mâché for added strength and to provide fixing tabs.

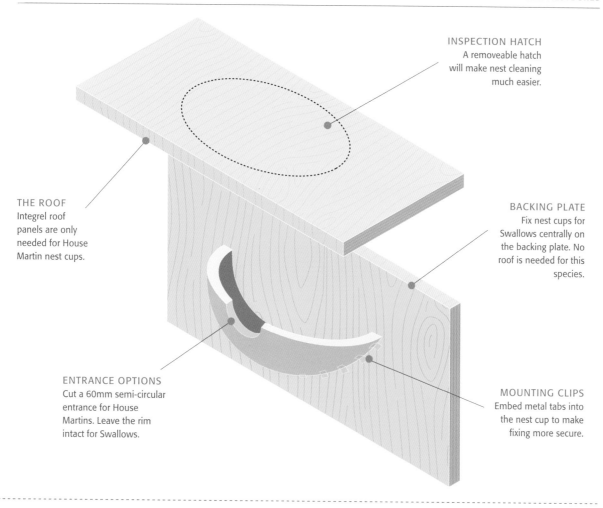

INSPECTION HATCH
A removeable hatch will make nest cleaning much easier.

THE ROOF
Integrel roof panels are only needed for House Martin nest cups.

BACKING PLATE
Fix nest cups for Swallows centrally on the backing plate. No roof is needed for this species.

ENTRANCE OPTIONS
Cut a 60mm semi-circular entrance for House Martins. Leave the rim intact for Swallows.

MOUNTING CLIPS
Embed metal tabs into the nest cup to make fixing more secure.

To finish the nest cup, continue adding layers of papier mâché to completely encase the metal strip.

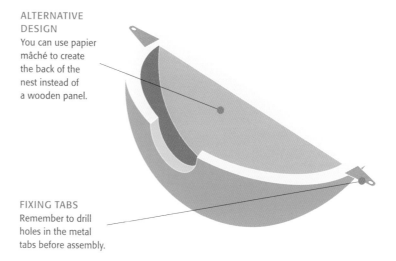

ALTERNATIVE DESIGN
You can use papier mâché to create the back of the nest instead of a wooden panel.

FIXING TABS
Remember to drill holes in the metal tabs before assembly.

PAPER AND GLUE METHOD

The traditional way of making papier mâché is to build up layers of torn newspaper strips over a mould, gluing each layer with a mix of flour and water, until you reach the required thickness. Today, an easier alternative is to use PVA glue for your adhesive as this will be more waterproof when dry.

Materials you need for this method are:

● A smooth plastic ball or blown-up balloon to act as your mould.
● PVA glue.
● Torn strips of newspaper.
● Vaseline for greasing the mould.
● Thin metal tabs for fixing the cup to a backboard.

STEP-BY-STEP INSTRUCTIONS

● Blow up a balloon or use a plastic ball of approximately 120mm diameter for your internal mould.
● Cover the mould in Vaseline to ease separation from the dry nest cup.
● Start pasting strips of newspaper (approximately 3cm wide and

MAKING NESTS WITH A MOULD

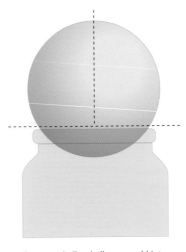

Place your ball or balloon mould into a jar or vase to hold it secure while pasting on strips of paper. When all the layers are dry, cut the papier mâché in half to remove the mould and then neatly trim the bottom edge for a better fit on the backing board.

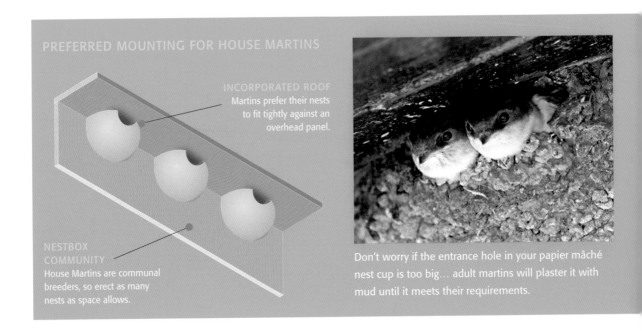

PREFERRED MOUNTING FOR HOUSE MARTINS

INCORPORATED ROOF
Martins prefer their nests to fit tightly against an overhead panel.

NESTBOX COMMUNITY
House Martins are communal breeders, so erect as many nests as space allows.

Don't worry if the entrance hole in your papier mâché nest cup is too big… adult martins will plaster it with mud until it meets their requirements.

10cm in length) to cover around three-quarters of the the ball or balloon shape. Glue the paper in different directions for each layer to give added strength. Keep pasting new layers until you reach a thickness of approx one centimetre.

● Fix metal tabs between layers of paper to help with fixing the nestbox to its backboard.

● Let the glue dry thoroughly before removing the mould. If you've used a ballooon, simply puncture it to release the cup nest.

● This method produces a large half-ball shape, so you can cut it in half to make two cup nests.

● Seal the inside and outside of the finished nest cup with waterproof varnish or PVA glue.

If you lack the time to make papier mâché nest cups, but would still like to help Swallows and House Martins in your area, then ensure they have a reliable source of mud so they can build their own nests. A unturned dustbin lid, sunk into an open patch of ground, will be large enough. Fill it with a mixture of water, soil, lime, clay and, if possible, some cattle dung. Keep a close eye on the mix and add water to maintain its moistness during dry periods.

To ensure it has a long life, seal the inside and outside of the finished nest cup with waterproof varnish or PVA glue.

TOP TIP
Place nests on north- and east-facing walls to attract martins. It may also help to smear the nest with mud, to mimic their own technique.

PREFERRED MOUNTING FOR SWALLOWS

AN OPEN TOP
Fix a Swallow nest centrally on a backing plate so the top remains open.

This nest made from mud, grass and other soft materials was built high inside a building, but with sufficient head-room to allow parent birds access to their hungry chicks.

HOUSE MARTIN
Delichon urbicum

IN SOME CASES YOUNGSTERS FROM THE SEASON'S FIRST
HOUSE MARTIN BROOD WILL HELP TO FEED A SUBSEQUENT FAMILY.

19mm

13mm

You can cater for the needs of nesting House Martins in two ways – by providing suitable locations for them to construct their own nests with mud or by providing an artificial nest cup (either papier mâché or a commercially produced alternative).

CAREFUL POSITIONING
House Martins have traditionally built nests under ledges on cliffs, but as their name suggests, they have found that our homes make very acceptable altenatives. They will usually seek out houses where there are deep eaves to shelter their nests.

A nest of mud needs to adhere strongly to the wall, so a rough surface is better than a smooth one. If your walls are smooth, try hammering in a series of masonry nails about 12cm below the eaves to aid nest attachment.

House Martins will often build their nests above doors or windows and this can annoy some householders who are constantly having to clean off bird droppings while the youngsters are in the nest. To avoid this problem, it is worth placing an artificial nestbox on a part of the house without windows, as martins can be attracted to build alongside.

MODIFICATIONS FOR MARTINS
The basic 'quarter ball' shape of a papier mâché nest needs to be modified slightly for House Martins as they favour a much smaller entrance than Swallows. When the papier mâché has hardened, cut a semi-circular hole approximately 60cm in diameter in the top edge. Don't worry if your cutting is not too precise – the birds will plaster mud into the entrance to ensure it is the correct size.

FACT FILE

HOW COMMON:
Around 510,000 breeding pairs.

WHERE THEY LIVE:
Found in all parts of Britain and Ireland, but only in small numbers in NW Scotland.

NESTING DENSITY:
A colonial nester, so you can fix as many nests as space allows.

NESTBOX TYPE:
A special design nest made from papier mâché or other man-made material with hole entrance.

NESTBOX LOCATION:
Under sheltered eaves on houses or other man-made structures.

HOW OFTEN THEY BREED:
Twice a year, but third broods possible.

NEST MATERIALS:
Mud cup lined with vegetable matter and feathers.

EGGS:
4–5 white eggs.

INCUBATION PERIOD:
14–16 days – by both parents.

NESTLINGS:
19–25 days before fledging.

CALENDAR	J	F	M	A	M	J	J	A	S	O	N	D
EGG LAYING:												
NESTLINGS:												

▲ Adult House Martins will plaster mud around the entrance of a nest cup until it meets their requirements.

KEEP CHICKS PROTECTED

If your home lacks deep eaves, fix a roof panel (approx 120mm wide) to the backboard of each papier mâché nest to give the nestlings some protection from the elements (see exploded view diagram on page 129). Your nest cup needs to be attached to the backboard and roof panel with metal tabs or glued strips of paper

Make the joins as waterproof as possible to prevent rain getting into the nest chamber and once the glue is dry, cover the nest and paper tabs with waterproof varnish.

Drill holes in the backboard or roof panel and attach to the house with screws or wingnuts. This will allow you to remove the nest for thorough cleaning when you are safely back at ground level. To maximise your chances of attracting House Martins, which naturally nest in colonies, build and fix as many nestboxes as possible. Even if they ignore your man-made efforts, they may just start building mud nests alongside!

House Martins have traditionally built nests under ledges on cliffs, but as their name suggests, they have found that our homes make very acceptable altenatives.

SWALLOW
Hirundo rustica

NEST-BUILDING AND PROVIDING FOOD FOR MULTIPLE FAMILIES
CAN BE EXHAUSTING FOR ADULT SWALLOWS.

20mm

14mm

FACT FILE

HOW COMMON:
Around 760,000 breeding territories.

WHERE THEY LIVE:
Widespread, particularly in lowland
farming areas. Absent or scarce only
in NW Scotland.

NESTBOX TYPE:
Open cup nest made from papier
mâché or other man-made material.

NESTBOX LOCATION:
Generrally inside barns or other
buildings, on ledges or under rafters.

HOW OFTEN THEY BREED:
Twice a year, but third broods possible.

NEST MATERIALS:
Cup lined with feathers.

EGGS:
4–5 white eggs.

INCUBATION PERIOD:
14–16 days – mainly by female.

NESTLINGS:
19–25 days before fledging.

When Swallows return from southern Africa in late April they will seek out
potential nest sites in barns and other buildings in rural areas, particularly those
near water. They will build their mud nests on ledges inside a building, and
sometimes this 'ledge' can be as minimal as a projecting nail.

CALENDAR	J	F	M	A	M	J	J	A	S	O	N	D
EGG LAYING:												
NESTLINGS:												

▲ Swallows construct their own mud nests on ledges inside buildings where they will be protected from bad weather.

LIFE ON THE LEDGE

You can increase nesting opportunities for this species by fixing ledges to walls or roofing timbers high in a roof space. It is a good idea to glue beading to the edge of your ledge to help keep the Swallow's nest in place.

Swallows like to nest as high as possible to minimise any threat to their offspring, but they will utilise low sheds as well as large barns. The most important factor governing their choice is guaranteed open access, so it is important to make sure there is always an open door or window for them to fly through.

PLENTY OF HEAD-ROOM

Swallows will happily take over a papier mâché nest (120mm to 130mm diameter), or a commercially produced alternative. Ideally you will be able to fix the nest cup's wooden backboard onto a wall about 100mm below roof level, leaving the top completely clear.

DID YOU KNOW?

A UK Swallow's return journey to South Africa or Namibia takes about six weeks. Flying in daylight, they can cover up to 320 km (200 miles) each day. At night they roost in huge flocks in reed-beds at traditional stop-over spots. It is believed that this helps the young birds to remember significant landmarks that will help them navigate on the return journey.

UK BIRD SPECIES THAT WILL USE ARTIFICIAL STRUCTURES

Birds have adapted to the loss of natural nesting locations by occupying pylons, platforms, tunnels and other constructions made by humans in many different habitats throughout the United Kingdom.

This book has focused on bird species that regularly use nestboxes of a fairly standard design, but there are many more that will take advantage of other types of artificial nest site. Many of these structures, such as platforms, rafts and nesting tunnels, are beyond what is suitable for a typical garden but they are ideal for nature reserves and for other sites where such birds may choose to breed.

Nest platforms, for example, can be attached to tall buildings to support nesting Peregrines, a species that has increased its use of urban areas over recent years. Rafts can be placed in flooded gravel pits to attract nesting terns, and baskets can be used for Long-eared Owls in areas of suitable woodland habitat.

Although this guide does not include details for building these different types of artificial site, it provides some pointers and you will be able to find more detailed instructions and designs on the internet.

NEST TUNNELS

Nest tunnels are boxes sited on or under the ground, some of which have a nest box at the end and some of which don't. They can comprise a single tunnel with a nestbox, such as the design used for Kingfisher, or be made up of a whole series of tunnels placed into an artificial bank, as is the case for a Sand Martin colony.

Other species that can be attracted to use a nesting tunnel include Storm Petrel, Puffin, Shelduck and Wheatear.

Some birds, notably Kingfisher and Sand Martin, prefer to excavate their own nesting tunnel or will extend a tunnel beyond the artificial section that has been provided. In such cases you will need to make sure that the substrate into which the tunnel has been positioned will not collapse if the bird decides to do some excavating of its own. In the case of Sand Martin, the tunnels should be filled with sand, which the birds will then remove when they arrive at the breeding colony during spring. Artificial tunnels should slope upwards gently from the entrance in order to allow for drainage; this is particularly important if the tunnel is constructed from an artificial and nonporous material.

RAFTS AND ISLANDS

Artificial islands and rafts are ideal for waterbirds like various divers, grebes, geese and terns, providing a nest site that can be positioned away from the bank and the attentions of most terrestrial predators. Rafts are best suited to sites with deeper water, while artificial islands can be created where the water is shallow enough to allow their construction.

Building a raft or artificial island is a substantial task, but not beyond a group of volunteers wishing to add new nesting opportunities to a site. Given the investment

MANDARIN: LARGE HOLE ENTRANCE
Several species of wildfowl are happy to use nestboxes, though they vary in their preferences. The decorative Mandarin, which was brought to Britain from China to enhance wildfowl collections, has now established itself in the wild where it can find breeding sites near water. Ideally, large boxes for this species will sit about a metre above ground level.

involved it is worth checking to see if a particular waterbody is likely to hold or attract the bird species that it is aimed at. You also need to consider which other species are present and whether they might take over the raft instead. If, for example, you are building a raft to attract nesting terns, then you might want to place a chicken wire fence around the edge of the raft to prevent the local Canada Geese from taking it over. The chicken wire will also offer protection against predators like American Mink.

Rafts typically consist of a sturdy frame, to which are attached floats – welded steel tanks make the best floats – and other fixings. The surface of the raft is then covered with soil, gravel and/or ballast, the amount of which will need to be adjusted until the raft floats at the correct level. The choice of material for the surface of the raft will also be determined by the target species, though gravel suits many species. The raft will also need to be anchored in place so that it protects both the birds and other users of the site.

OSPREY: BASKET

Fish-eating Ospreys disappeared as a breeding species in Britain in 1916 and almost 40 years elapsed before a pair of Scandinavian birds recolonised Scotland naturally. Ospreys prefer to breed close to other nests, so their population spread was very slow until a new colony was established at Rutland Water with birds intoduced from the Scottish Highlands. Erecting wooden platforms on top of tall posts in secure locations and where food is plentiful has played a big part in encouraging Ospreys to breed in new areas.

BASKETS AND PLATFORMS

A number of bird species will make use of old nests, built by other species, rather than necessarily construct one of their own. Long-eared Owl is a good example of such a species, but others include Kestrel and Hobby. Some larger birds of prey may benefit from a helping hand, perhaps from the provision of a nesting platform attached to a tall building (Peregrine) or tall post (Osprey). In fact, the erection of such platforms has probably played an important role in the successful expansion of both Osprey and Peregrine populations here in the UK.

As you might expect, larger platforms need a strong frame and, if positioned on top of a tall pole, particular care will be needed to make sure that the pole is stable and placed very firmly into the ground.

For smaller species, including small birds of prey like Kestrel and Long-eared Owl, wicker basket can provide the necessary foundations for a nest. The basket should be attached securely to a suitable location, before an old crow nest is used to line the basket and form the platform onto which the Kestrel or owl can lay its eggs. In the case of Long-eared Owl, the wicker basket should have a diameter of 30–40 cm, a depth of 15–20 cm and nearly vertical sides. Wicker baskets will last a lot longer if they are varnished before being put out. Only use twigs for the lining, as sawdust or shavings will become waterlogged..

OTHER NESTING OPPORTUNITIES

It is possible to provide other nesting opportunities within your garden by thinking about the vegetation that is present. For example, faggots or bundles of sticks may be placed within a climber, hedge or shrub to provide somewhere for a Wren or Robin to build its nest. The addition of a platform or tray to the inside of a shed or outbuilding to which there is ready access, may encourage a Blackbird or Robin.

Alternatively, you can manage your garden trees and shrubs to produce 'natural' nest sites. Many thrushes and finches like to nest where several smaller branches emerge from a larger one. By pruning a shrub you can encourage the growth of such shoots, which then form a cradle into which a nest can be constructed. Perhaps you may be persuaded to plant a creeper against a wall because of the nesting opportunities it will provide once it has matured. You can also enlarge the entrance of a natural cavity or add a drainage hole to one that would suitable were it not flooded with rainwater.

There are opportunities to help nesting birds in other ways, perhaps by providing material that can be used to line a nest, such as wool or the fur from a dog that has been recently groomed. The provision of appropriate supplementary foods during the winter months may help birds to get into breeding condition and, as we have seen elsewhere in this book, adopting a wildlife-friendly approach to managing your garden may help to boost populations of the insects and other invertebrates on which many small birds feed their chicks.

Whatever you chose to do to help your nesting birds, don't forget the role that nest monitoring can play in helping researchers and conservationists understand why bird populations change. For example, by contributing to the BTO's Nest Record Scheme you can add to our knowledge, sharing the details of the nesting attempts made in your garden and in the nestboxes and other structures that you have created for nesting birds. To find out more, please visit the BTO website, www.bto.org.

BLACKBIRD: PLATFORM (ROOFED)

Though most Blackbirds will construct nests in the forks of trees or bushes, they will sometimes build on a shelf or ledge of an old building (as shown in the photograph above). They may also be tempted if you provide a large platform type nestbox in your garden. This needs to be completely open at the front, but with a roof to provide weather protection. Make sure the box is hidden in vegetation to escape the attention of predators.

COMMON TERN: RAFT OR ISLAND

Many nature reserves and country parks with larger lakes now boast tern rafts in an attempt to offer migrant Common Terns a safe place to raise their families. Rafts need to be stable enough to withstand high winds and choppy waves and in many areas they need to be enclosed with polycarbonate side panels to prevent predators such as American Mink clambering aboard.

Terns will make scrape nests in gravel placed over the surface of a raft and if the colony is large enough the adults are feisty enoughy to deter most aerial predators.

MORE WAYS TO HELP WILDLIFE

Providing refuges for hibernating Hedgehogs, Common Dormice and toads, roosting bats and a myriad of insects will help boost biodiversity in your garden.

Once your garden is stocked with all the bird nestboxes it can accommodate, you might like to explore other construction projects to help wildlife. The sad fact is that many British species, such as Hedgehogs, bats, frogs and toads, plus a wide range of insects, are struggling for survival and need just as much human aid as wild birds.

A WINTER REFUGE FOR HEDGEHOGS

Keen gardeners should do all they can to attract Hedgehogs as they eat slugs and other 'pest' insects. Around November they will start to prospect for places in which to hibernate – this may be a compost heap, a heap of leaves or a pile of loosely stacked logs.

Depending on the severity of the winter, Hedgehogs may not wake again till mid to late March, which means they are in a vulnerable state for a long period, particularly those that chose outdoor locations. Providing a safer nesting box can make a big difference to survival rates.

There are many ready-made Hedgehog boxes for sale, but if you want to construct your own, there are a few basic features you should incorporate:

- To deter predators entering the nesting chamber, construct a long entrance tunnel, but ensure it is big enough to admit the largest Hedgehogs.

- Build the box and tunnel from outdoor-quality 15mm plywood or offcuts of sawn timber. Use water-based preservatives on both sides of each panel.
- Fit a removeable roof to the nesting chamber to make cleaning easier.
- Fit wooden battens below the floor to raise the nesting chamber off the ground and drill holes into the base to improve drainage.
- Situate the box in a quiet corner of the garden, and cover with leaves and other garden debris to confuse would-be predators.

DORMICE HIBERNATION BOXES

Dormice are mainly found in broadleaf and mixed woodland, as well as in wild gardens and orchards, but the large-scale destruction of suitable habitats has led to serious population declines.

Dormice hunt mainly at night during the summer months and rest during the day in nests, which are usually made of moss, grasses, leaves and small twigs. Ideally, these nests will be hidden in holes in trees or in thickets, but if such sites are not available, dormice may also compete with birds for nesting holes.

To help them, you can buy special boxes, known as dreys, where they can rest during their active

WINTER REFUGE FOR HEDGEHOGS

Attract Hedgehogs to your garden by putting out small amounts of dog food, never bread and milk. Right: The month of April is the only safe time to clean out boxes: at this time most Hedgehogs will have woken from hibernation but are not yet ready to mate or to look for maternity nests.

A RETREAT FOR THE DAYTIME

In the summer months, Dormice forage at night and spend daylight hours asleep in tree holes or other secure spots. More research is needed to determine what is the best height to locate nestboxes for them, but in all cases the entrance hole should be situated facing the supporting tree (inset picture).

months or hibernate, living for up to six months off fat reserves built up during the summer.

If you fancy making your own boxes for Dormice, use our template for a bird nestbox with a small entrance holes but make the depth at least 230mm. The diameter of the entrance hole needs to be 26mm. Fix a batten above the entrance hole and another at the base of that panel, so that when you come to position the box the entrance hole faces the tree to which it is being attached. The battens ensure there is a space for the Dormouse to climb between the tree trunk and the box.

Ideally, whatever height you place the box, you can find a location where honeysuckle or another climber provides a natural ladder to it. Dormice are legally protected, so you will need to get a licence to examine nestboxes.

WOODEN BOXES FOR BATS

Bats need a range of roosting sites, including summer daytime roosts, winter hibernation and breeding sites. You can help them find a suitable roost by putting up a simple bat box, particularly if you've observed bats hunting for insects near your garden.

If you have the space to accommodate several boxes, get them facing in different directions to provide a range of conditions. Place your boxes as high as possible in sheltered sunny places, either on trees or buildings. If fixing to the house, aim to put boxes as close to the eaves as possible.

A range of commercially available bat boxes is available, but if you want to make your own, then aim to create ones that are sufficiently well insulated to keep temperature and humidity changes to a minimum.

Successful boxes are generally rectangular (max height 340mm, width 135mm). As bats prefer to enter the box through a narrow entrance groove (no more than 20mm wide), the top of the box needs to be deeper (around 100mm) than the bottom.

▲ There are several designs for bat boxes which you can try making, either for daytime refuges or places to hibernate.

Bats need textured wood to cling to, so avoid using plywood or MDF for your boxes, and because they are very sensitive to chemicals do not use preservatives. A bat box cannot be opened legally without a licence. For more information on bats and the law call the Bat Helpline (0345 1300 228).

INSECT HOTELS

As mentioned earlier in the book, birds will only thrive in habitats that are biologically diverse, so looking after insects should be a high priority in all gardens. Not only will bees, hoverflies and other insects repay you by pollinating your plants, but other species will contribute to the natural predation of garden pests, such as aphids and greenfly.

INSECT REFUGES –
LARGE AND SMALL
The range of manufactured 'bug
houses' grows ever larger and many
can be located where they can easily
be monitored by children. Right:
In larger gardens, you can create a
more substantial 'insect hotel' to
shelter the widest spread of species.

You can unleash your 'hidden sculptor' by making
an 'insect hotel': a multi-chambered tower of varied
materials to create potential habitats for garden-friendly
insects. Placed near flowering or scented plants, these
'insect hotels' provide over-wintering habitats for
ladybirds and lacewings and a home for solitary bees
(non-aggressive pollinators), and other beneficial insects
during both winter and summer. Gaps at ground level
can shelter toads and Hedgehogs.

Assemble a collection of natural materials such as
straw, dry grass, loose bark, pine cones, bamboo and
other hollow plant stems, plus human products such
as corrugated cardboard, wooden pallets, bricks and tiles.

Start your construction by placing bricks on the
ground in your chosen location where it can catch
the morning sun. Cover these with roof tiles or a
wooden pallet to create a shady, damp area that will
appeal to frogs and toads. Then place a pallet onto
the bricks as the first storey of your tower.

Next, fill the gaps in the pallet with dead wood
and loose bark to provide a range of crevices,
tunnels and cosy beds for beetles, centipedes and
spiders. To cater for solitary bees, make a series of
tubes out of bamboo, reeds and drilled logs, and
if you are a wine drinker, you can also drill holes
through unwanted corks!

Keep adding new layers up to a height of about
one metre, but ensure the whole construction is

PROVIDE SAFE PLACES TO HIBERNATE
A garden that boasts a pond should also offer frogs (left) and toads safe places in which to hibernate. This home-made hibernaculum is simply a hole in the ground, partially filled with a jumble of sticks and bricks to create hidey-holes at different levels. Plastic drainpipes give access to these chambers. Make a roof from a sheet of tin or wooden planks.

stable in case children try to use it as a climbing frame. It is worth adding a roof to keep your bug house relatively dry. If old roof tiles are not available, use old planks covered with roofing felt.

Manufacturers of garden-related products have created a wide range of refuges for bees and other insects, so even if you don't have space for an 'insect hotel' you can opt to downsize.

WINTER REFUGES FOR AMPHIBIANS

Frogs and toads like to hibernate in cool, dark and damp shelters, safely away from predators. If you have a pond in your garden it is possible that some frogs may hibernate in the mud at the bottom, but others will spend the winter on land, tucked away below ground level if possible. You can create the ideal winter shelter (technically known as a hibernaculum) very simply.

Choose a sheltered, shady spot, preferably close to a pool, to dig a flat-bottomed hole about 450mm deep. Once that is done, place stones and logs into the hole. Overlap them to create spaces at different levels that can be occupied by amphibians.

Continue the process above ground level until you have a mound and cap it with some planks to create a roof. Cover this with the soil you originally excavated from the hole, but ensure there are several holes at the side of the mound where frogs and toads can gain access to the chambers below.

MORE THINGS YOU CAN DO TO HELP BIRDS

By contributing your sightings of birds and other garden wildlife to national projects run by the British Trust for Ornithology you can increase our understanding of the most pressing conservation issues.

The fact you've bought this book with the intention of building and installing nestboxes demonstrates a desire to do something positive to help birds or other forms of wildlife. Your feeling of satisfaction is likely to grow once your nestboxes have been occupied and, later, when fledgling birds visit your bird feeders.

You may then ask yourself 'Is there anything more I can do for my local birds?' The simple answer is 'yes' and there are several options to choose from, depending on the time you can spare and your bird identification skills.

BTO GARDEN BIRDWATCH

A natural first step is to take part in BTO Garden BirdWatch, a weekly survey of garden wildlife and one of the best supported 'citizen science' projects in the UK (www.bto.org/gbw).

This is one of many British Trust for Ornithology projects where volunteers count or survey birds and work in partnership with BTO scientists to provide unbiased information about birds and their habitats. The information collected by BTO volunteers provides evidence that informs the decisions made by those managing the land or involved in conservation.

Many householders already keep simple records of birds they see using their gardens throughout the year.

The collection of such information is incredibly useful and, if carried out in a systematic manner, these weekly observations of birds (or indeed other garden wildlife) can prove very valuable for researchers.

Garden BirdWatch monitors the changing fortunes of birds and other garden wildlife through its country-wide network of volunteers. Their weekly observations have charted the decline of the House Sparrow, the rise of the Woodpigeon and, among other things, revealed that urban birds get up later than their rural counterparts.

The project is self-funded; in return for a small annual fee, participants in the scheme receive a free book when they join, plus a quarterly magazine that reports on what is happening in gardens up and down the country, including unusual observations and interesting behaviour.

GARDEN WILDLIFE HEALTH

Very occasionally you may come across a bird in your garden that either shows signs of ill health or is found dead, perhaps having collided with a window. Garden Wildlife Health (www.gardenwildlifehealth.org) enables observers to submit information through a simple web-form on birds found sick or dead in their garden.

It is important to understand the impacts of disease and other causes of mortality and to be able

▲ Once hooked by watching garden birds, why not join in national surveys devoted to monitoring species in the breeding season?

to provide appropriate advice that can help reduce the impacts of disease.

BTO NEST RECORD SCHEME

The Nest Record Scheme gathers vital information on the breeding success of Britain's birds by asking volunteers to find and follow the progress of individual nests. Anyone can be a nest recorder and if you have put up a nestbox in your garden then you are ideally placed to make a contribution by monitoring its progress.

Registering to take part is easy and there are lots of resources to help you get started; visit the web site

(www.bto.org/nrs) or request a Nest Record Scheme starter pack by e-mailing info@bto.org or by writing to The Nest Records Officer, BTO, The Nunnery, Thetford, Norfolk, IP24 2PU.

As with all BTO surveys, the welfare of the birds comes first, and therefore all nest recorders follow the Nest Record Scheme Code of Conduct, a protocol designed to ensure that monitoring a nest does not influence its outcome.

The data collected for NRS are used to produce trends in breeding performance, which help us to identify species that may be declining because of problems at the nesting stage. These trends are updated every year and also allow us to measure the impacts that pressures, such as climate change, have on birds and their breeding success.

Monitoring the progress of your nest involves making several visits to the nestbox to count the number of eggs and the number of chicks. By following the Code of Conduct you won't disturb the breeding birds and you'll collect key information about the breeding attempt, including whether or not it was ultimately successful.

To get a complete nationwide picture of breeding success, it is equally important to report when nestboxes are not used. Keep checking your box until the end of

August: most nestbox species don't fledge chicks until the beginning of June, and some species may have a second brood in the summer.

Recording events in nests is fascinating, and may even become addictive, so be warned! Even seasoned nestbox watchers can be surprised by what they find. The author of the previous version of this book, Chris du Feu, once found a Wren nest in a box already occupied by a roosting Hornet. Elsewhere, a successful Tawny Owl nestbox was used for three successful broods of Stock Dove in one season.

THE KEY EVENTS IN A BIRD'S BREEDING CYCLE

Nest building: Look for signs of birds collecting twigs, moss and other vegetation. Keep your distance when nest building is taking place.

First egg date: Make afternoon visits to identify the day the first egg is laid. Small birds generally lay one egg a day until the clutch is complete, with most doing so in the morning. So, a new egg found in the afternoon will be most likely to be the egg of that day.

Incubation checks: Examine the nest during incubation to discover the total number of eggs laid. Another visit, nearer hatching, will allow you to record the number of surviving eggs being incubated.

Post-hatching: Visit two or three days after hatching to record the number of eggs hatched.

Check on nestlings: Two-thirds of the way through the nestling period, check the nest to record how many nestlings have survived.

Fledging date: Establish the fledging date by watching from a distance. If you get too close you may trigger the young birds to leave the nest prematurely,

something that is an inbuilt anti-predator response.

After fledging: Record the number of unhatched eggs and any remaining dead young birds left behind in the nest. Bear in mind that some dead young may already have been removed by a parent bird.

Follow-up: For species that are multi-brooded, check nest sites on a weekly basis for a second clutch and then repeat the produces given above.

▶ More and more active birdwatchers now log their sightings on the BirdTrack app. Not only does it help them manage their own bird records, but all the information is automatically available to researchers involved in migration and other studies.

BREEDING BIRD SURVEY

If you catch the recording bug, the BTO has many other surveys you might consider joining. The BTO/JNCC/ RSPB Breeding Bird Survey (BBS) is the main scheme for monitoring how the populations of more than 100 of the UK's common breeding birds change over time.

To contribute to this survey you will need to be able to identify birds by sight, or by their calls and songs. After being allocated a survey square near to your home you will be asked to make three visits between April and June. The first visit enables you to record the various habitats present and work out the best route to follow on foot. On the other two visits, which generally take about an hour and a half to complete, you'll be recording the birds that you see and hear.

Wild bird populations are an important indicator of the health of the countryside, and knowing to what extent bird populations are increasing or decreasing is fundamental to bird conservation.For more information on this survey visit (www.bto.org/bbs).

BIRDTRACK

BirdTrack is a partnership project, involving BTO, RSPB, Birdwatch Ireland, the Scottish Ornithologists' Club and the Welsh Ornithological Society, that looks at migration movements and distributions of birds throughout Britain and Ireland.

If you go for walks in the countryside or visit nature reserves and other sites to birdwatch, then the BirdTrack app (available free on both Android and Apple) provides you with a powerful 'notebook tool' for keeping and managing your birdwatching records.

The beauty of the system, which can also be used via a computer at home, is that your records are – with your permission – also made available to BTO researchers, studying bird migration and populations, and to County Bird Recorders and others involved in bird conservation. BirdTrack (www.birdtrack.net) provides facilities for you to store and manage your own records, enabling you to keep a list of what you have seen, where and in what numbers.

APPENDICES

FURTHER READING AND USEFUL ADDRESSES

Collins BTO Guide to British Birds

by Paul Sterry and Paul Stancliffe. (2015).
Published by William Collins

Boasting more than 1,200 images, this book is undoubtedly the best photographic guide for identifying breeding and wintering birds, plus passage migrants, in Britain. Apart from helpful identification advice, the book contains abundance maps based on the latest BTO research.

A Field Guide to Monitoring Nests

by James Ferguson-Lees, Richard Castell and David Leech. (2011).
Published by BTO Books

The Bible for anyone involved in monitoring nests for research and conservation purposes. Contains a wealth of information on 146 British and Irish species, plus tips on fieldcraft, legislation and the BTO Nest Record Scheme. Has photographs showing nests, eggs and young of all common UK species.

Garden Birds & Other Wildlife

by Kate Risely and Clare Simm. (2016).
Published by BTO Books

A detailed guide to 61 garden bird species, including key facts on their ecology and behaviour, plus ID guides to mammals, reptiles, amphibians, butterflies, dragonflies and bumblebees. There are also sections on bird behaviour and ecology and wildlife-friendly gardening.

Gardening for Birdwatchers

by Mike Toms (2008).
Published by BTO Books

This 96-page book provides useful advice for improving your garden for birds and other wildlife. In addition to information on where to site nest boxes, the well-illustrated text contains detailed planting designs and lists of plants beneficial to garden wildlife.

RHS Companion to Wildlife Gardening
by Chris Baines. (2016).
Published by Frances Lincoln

 First published as How to Make a Wildlife Garden in 1985, this book helped to make wildlife a mainstream issue for gardeners and the public.
Now fully revised and updated by the author, this illustrated edition highlights the changes in garden wildlife over the past 30 years. It incorporates Royal Horticultural Society research, updated best practice and addresses a multitude of controversial conservation issues.

RSPB Gardening for Wildlife:
A Complete Guide to Nature Friendly
Gardening
(2nd ed) by Adrian Thomas. (2017).
Published by Bloomsbury Natural History

 Written in a friendly tone, this expanded and updated edition offers a huge amount of information. It reflects the latest research and developments in nature-friendly gardening and educates readers about the ecological principles involved. The catalogue of 500 best garden flowers, shrubs and trees for wildlife, now includes colour photos of every species.

RSPB Handbook of British Birds
(4th edition) by Peter Holden
and Tim Cleeves. (2014).
Published by Bloomsbury Natural History

 The updated fourth edition provides a 'biography' of each of the 280 commonest British bird species. Apart from covering all aspects of field identification, the text also provides information on behaviour, breeding biology, distribution, population, status, longevity and any other interesting facts about the species concerned. The updated rarities section features 26 additional species. The RSPB Handbook provides a complete, single source of basic information to our most familiar birds.

RSPB Handbook of Garden Wildlife
(2nd edition) by Peter Holden
and Geoffrey Abbott. (2017).
Published by Bloomsbury Natural History

 The second edition has been updated and expanded to offer comprehensive coverage of species now found in British gardens. Full of advice on attracting wildlife to your garden, the book also includes helpful guides to wildlife gardening projects. Every type of flora and fauna is covered, with each account covering identification, habits, characteristics, food and garden conservation.

RSPB My First Book of Garden Wildlife
by Mike Unwin. (2008).
Published by A & C Black

If you want to get children excited about wildlife close to home, the First Book series will be a good starting point. Attractive illustrations and lively text by a talented and knowledgeable author introduce young readers to 20 common garden animals, birds and insects in a fun question-and-answer format. Other books in the series cover garden birds and common insects.

The Wildlife Garden: The Essential Guide to Attracting Wildlife into Your Garden
by John Lewis-Stempel. (2014).
Published by How To Books

The author is a Country Life columnist and provides a succinct but detailed guide to attracting birds, butterflies and a whole array of other creatures into your garden – even if you only have a window box. Though devoid of photographs, this small book is full of information on what plants are best for wildlife, on how to make refuges for insects and homes for bats, on making a pool for frogs, all while adding scent and colour to your surroundings.

The Wildlife Trusts: Chris Packham's Back Garden Nature Reserve
by Chris Packham. (2015).
Published by Bloomsbury

This comprehensive new edition explains the best ways to attract wildlife to gardens and encourage it to stay there. Written in a light-hearted yet authoritative style, the guide is complemented by attractive photographs and illustrations and will encourage an interest in the natural world on the doorstep in readers of all ages.

The Wildlife Gardener: Creating a Haven for Birds, Bees and Butterflies
by Karen Bradbury. (2013).
Published by Kyle Books

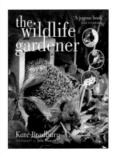

A book which helps you to create wildlife habitats in your very own garden, and is very handily split into sections on shelter, food and water. Kate gives advice on the best nectar and pollen plants to grow, dos and don'ts of bird feeding and organic methods of pest control. There are also 10 step-by-step projects that will help encourage wildlife into your garden, such as: creating a bumblebee nester, making a green roof and building a Hedgehog box. Also included is a mini field guide, which will help you to identify the birds and other creatures that you are likely to see in your garden.

Making Wildlife Ponds:
How to Create a Pond to Attract
Wildlife to Your Garden
by Jenny Steel. (2016).
Published by Brambely Books

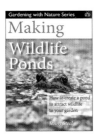

This third guide in the 'Gardening with Nature Series' is written by a plant ecologist and gives step-by-step advice on where, when and how to create and maintain a pond to enrich the wildlife in your garden. It is not a large book, but the most important points about attracting insects, amphibians, birds and animals with natural-looking water features are delivered in straightforward language.

The Pond Specialist: Designing, Building, Improving and Maintaining Ponds and Water Features
by A & G Bridgewater. (2016).
Published by Creative Homeowner

This book is aimed at anyone who is thinking of building a pond from scratch or who needs to know how to keep an existing water feature at its best. The book starts with the basics of assessing the garden, checking the site, planning and preparation, tools and materials and electrical wiring and safety. The authors discuss different types of pond – not just those for wildlife – and how they can be created, maintained and enhanced.

USEFUL ADDRESSES

BIRD ORGANISATIONS

Action For Swifts
actionforswifts.blogspot.co.uk
A blog about Swifts with some useful resources and links.

Barn Owl Trust
www.barnowltrust.org.uk
Dedicated to conserving the Barn Owl and its environment. Website contains detailed information on building and erecting owl boxes indoors and outdoors. Also sells boxes for different owl species.

British Trust for Ornithology
www.bto.org
Share your interest in birds with others by being part of the British Trust for Ornithology (BTO). Volunteer surveyors, members and staff work in partnership to provide unbiased information about birds and their habitats. Website has lots of accessible information about birds, including identification videos to help you get to grips identifying different species.

Hawk & Owl Trust
http://hawkandowl.org
Working to conserve of birds of prey and their habitats. Website promotes nestbox sales and an adopt-a-box scheme.

Royal Society for the Protection of Birds
www.rspb.org.uk
With more than a million members, the RSPB manages a wide range of wildlife

reserves in the UK as well as supporting overseas conservation. Website provides basic information about making, siting and maintaining nestboxes, while the online shop sells a wide variety of bird and insect boxes.

Swift Conservation

www.swift-conservation.org

An advice service for anyone wanting to build and install nestboxes for Swifts.

OTHER WILDLIFE GROUPS

Amphibian and Reptile Groups UK

www.arguk.org

A charity set up to promote the conservation of native amphibian and reptiles and their environment by promoting and supporting a network of more than 45 independent Amphibian and Reptile Groups (ARGs) across the UK.

Bat Conservation Trust

www.bats.org.uk

Supports more than 100 local bat groups and 6,000 members and works with volunteers, scientists, industry and government on a range of projects concerned with the conservation of bats and the landscapes on which they depend. Has advice on making bat boxes.

British Hedgehog Preservation Society

www.britishhedgehogs.org.uk

Offers help and advice to those with sick, injured or orphaned Hedgehogs and maintains a list of rehabilitators in the UK. Has advice and designs for building a Hedgehog box.

Buglife

www.buglife.org.uk

Devoted to the conservation of all invertebrates. As well as developing knowledge about the conservation of invertebrates, it supports the efforts of other organisations and undertakes practical conservation projects and wildlife surveys.

Froglife

www.froglife.org

A national wildlife charity committed to the conservation of amphibians and reptiles – frogs, toads, newts, snakes and lizards – and saving the habitats they depend on. Lots of information and useful advice.

Mammal Society

www.mammal.org.uk

Leading efforts to collect and share information on mammals, encourage research about their ecology and distribution and to contribute meaningfully to efforts to conserve them. Website provides information on the UK's mammal species.

Wildlife Trusts

www.wildlifetrusts.org

A membership organisation of more than 800,000 supporters made up of a federation of Wildlife Trusts around the UK. In addition to managing 95,000 hectares of land in its own network of nature reserves, the Trust works with land-owners, businesses and local fishing industries to try to achieve positive change for wildlife.

ACKNOWLEDGEMENTS AND PICTURE CREDITS

ABOUT THE AUTHOR

David Cromack has been a long-term member of the British Trust for Ornithology and contributes monthly sightings to the Wetland Bird Survey. He is currently chairman of Peterborough Bird Club.

A professional journalist for the bulk of his working life, David was editor of the market-leading monthly Bird Watching magazine for almost 20 years, as well as editing and publishing Birds Illustrated magazine for six years. Other titles he has edited include Natural World, on behalf of The Wildlife Trusts, Go Birdwatching and Bird Art & Photography.

Together with his wife Hilary, David bought Buckingham Press Ltd in 2000 in order to continue publishing the long-established Birdwatcher's Yearbook on an annual basis. They also published the Best Birdwatching Sites series of guides to selected UK birding counties, along with the ID Insights Pocket Card guides to birds, butterflies and dragonflies.

ACKNOWLEDGEMENTS

This volume is merely the latest in a continuous lineage of BTO Nestbox guides, starting with the first in 1952 by Edwin Cohen and Bruce Campbell, with subsequent editions being edited by Jim Flegg, David Glue and Chris du Feu.

I am very conscious that my birding credentials pale into insignificance compared to my predecessors, so it has been reassuring that Chris du Feu has kept a fatherly watch over the development of the new book. I am very grateful to his many helpful suggestions and general encouragement.

Much of the material is based on that written by Chris for the 2003 edition (with input from other BTO staff such as Graham Appleton, Peter Beavan, Nick Carter and David Glue), but this time around we have added material on wildlife gardening and other wildlife to attract the interest of new audiences.

Overseeing the whole project, as well as sourcing photographic images, has been Jeff Baker, newly retired from his position as Head of Marketing for the British Trust for Ornithology. Other BTO staff to have made invaluable contributions are Mike Toms, Dave Leech and Carl Barrimore. Simon Gillings generated the distribution maps (using Bird Atlas 2007–11 data).

The design concept and elegant page designs are the work of Tom Sayer (tomsayerdesign.co.uk) and Nigel Hawtin provided the nestbox construction illustrations. Paul Sterry (Nature Photographers Ltd) supplied all photographs of eggs.

Barn Owls and Swifts are two species that have benefited from the work of many people and as a result we now have a better idea of their nesting requirements. I am grateful that Peter Wilkinson (Barn Owl), Dick Newell, Jake Allsop and Edward Mayer (Swift) have been kind enough to share their expertise with me and our readers.

EDITORIAL PRODUCTION

Author David Cromack
Managing Editor Jeff Baker
Art Director Tom Sayer
Illustrator Nigel Hawtin
Proof Readers Jeff Baker, Graham Evans, Dave Leech and Mike Toms
Printer Printer Trento, Italy

PHOTOGRAPHIC CREDITS

FRONT COVER

David Tipling: Nuthatch, Blue Tit, Great Tit chicks
NE Wildlife: Wren

ALL YOU NEED TO KNOW ABOUT NESTBOXES

Jeff Baker p19d, p20a, p22, p47

John Harding p32
David Cromack p38
Countryside Restoration Trust in Surrey p32b
Adrian Dancy p21
Edmund Fellowes p46a, p46b,
DIY Network p20b
Lev Dolgachov/Alamy Stock Photo p37
Vereniging Gierzwalvwbescherming p43
Tommy Holden p23
John Harding p34a
Keith Law/Alamy Stock Photo p13
Naturepix/Alamy Stock Photo p17
Jill Pakenham p18
Colin Paton p33b, p34b, p39, p40, p41, p42a
Mary Michael Patterson p19a
Robert Rendall p42b
Moss Taylor p19c, p19e
David Tipling p15, p19f, p25, p27, p29a, p30, p35, p45, p46c
Ken Woodgate p33a

NESTBOXES WITH SMALL-SIZED ENTRANCE HOLES

John Proudlock p59
Birdpix/Alamy Stock Photo p65a
Mark Bretherton/Alamy Stock Photo p63b
David Chapman/Alamy Stock Photo p69
Steven Faiers p65b
Edmund Fellowes p61b, p71
John Flowerday p53, p58
ImageBROKER/Alamy Stock Photo p70
Jonathan Plant/Alamy Stock Photo p61a
John Proudlock p54c, p68
Michael Schroeder/Alamy Stock Photo p63a
Moss Taylor p54b, p66, p67b
Mike Toms p67a
David Tipling p52, p55, p56, p57, p62
Duncan Usher/Alamy Stock Photo p54a

NESTBOXES WITH MEDIUM-SIZED ENTRANCE HOLES

Blickwinkel/Alamy Stock Photo p78a

Chris du Feu p81b

John Flowerday p77

John Harding p79, p81a

Sarah Kelman p80

John Proudlock p78b

NESTBOXES WITH LARGE-SIZED ENTRANCE HOLES

Sally Andrews/Alamy Stock Photo p92a

Edmund Fellowes p87

Chris du Feu p88b

Graham Giddens p89

David Hosking p93

Minden Pictures/Alamy Stock Photo p86

Howard Stockdale p91

Moss Taylor p90

Simon Thurgood p92b

Richard Winston p88a

SMALL OPEN-FRONTED NESTBOXES

Blickwinkel/Alamy Stock Photo p101, p105a

John Cranfield p100c

Liz Cutting p102

John Harding p106

Gray Images p99

Steve Nesbitt p104

NE Wildlife p103, p105b

Jill Pakenham p100b

David Tipling p98

David Waistell p100a

Dave Watts/Alamy Stock Photo p107

SPECIALIST NESTBOXES

John Cranfield p126a

Chris du Feu p128b, p129

Graham Giddens p127b

John Harding p130, p134, p135

Steven McGrath/Alamy Stock Photo p125

Alan Price p119a

Graham Roberts p113a

Neil Schofield p123

Colin Shawyer p126b, p127a

Swift Conservation p113c

Ulrich Tigges p110

David Tipling p131

Mike Toms p119b

Nick Upton p111, p113b

Doug Welch p133

Gordon Yates p117

MORE ABOUT NESTBOXES

Bhandol/Alamy Stock Photo p145

Mark Bretherton/Alamy Stock Photo p144

David Cromack p146b

Robert Harding/Alamy Stock Photo p144a

Jacobi Jayne & Company p146a

Linda Kennedy/Alamy Stock Photo p139

mammalpix/ Alamy Stock Photo p143b

Jill Pakenham p141a

Chris Park p141b

Roger Parkes/Alamy Stock Photo p147b

Lee Rentz/Alamy Stock Photo p140

Moss Taylor p147a

Tierotoagentur/Alamy Stock Photo p143a

David Tipling p149, p150, p151

BACK COVER

Mike Alsford: Nick Baker

David Tipling: Great Tit

QUICK INDEX